QUEENS WHO
DEFIED
THE ODDS

RESILIENCY IS NOT JUST SURVIVING BUT THRIVING

Dear Felix
Trust God from the
bottom of your heart and
let God direct your path
May this be a great season
in your life.
God is Faithful!
Love
Julieta

VISIONARY AUTHOR
CHERYL A.S. HURLEY

Table of Contents

Introduction

> "You may encounter many defeats, but you must not be defeated. In fact, it may be necessary to encounter the defeats, so you can know who you are, what you can rise from, how you can still come out of it." – **Maya Angelou**

How many of you have had dreams and goals that you set out to accomplish, only to have them interrupted with adversity of some type that literally—and I mean literally—knocked you off, or so you thought, the path that God had planned for your life? I'm talking about those situations or circumstances that left you standing with your mouth open, shocked in sheer disbelief, and you asked God, "What am I supposed to do NOW?" or What am I supposed to do with this?" or "There's no way I can bounce back from this!" Because your belief system whispered but was yelling, "IT'S JUST NOT POSSIBLE!!!" you almost gave up.

Sound familiar? Well, this, for me, was a part of the journey God began in my life a long time ago, except He didn't let me in on the secret that He was growing me through what I was going through. As men and women of faith, we often quote and some even preach Jeremiah 29:11, reminding us that God knows exactly what He's doing, that He has our lives all planned out, that He will provide for

1

us and take care of us, that He won't abandon us and He has plans to give us the future we hope for. And our response, often is... "But God – this?"

When God calls us to an assignment, He means business. In 2003, God spoke to me through His Word, in Isaiah 40:1, "Cheryl, I have called you to....'Comfort, yes, comfort My people!'" I paused and took note of the things I was doing and didn't fully connect that what I enjoyed doing was a call upon my life. Can I say mind blown! After acknowledging my life assignment, I began a long, arduous journey of growth - my going through. As I was an avid reader, one of my mentors, Dr. Robert E. Brown, introduced me to several influential books for my Growth Library. One of them was *The Assignment* by Dr. Mike Murdock. In particular, as I reflect on why this book was so transformational concerning 'my' life assignment, it was in discovering the rewards of the pain and how God would use it to unlock the flow of miracles in my life that moved me from merely surviving to thriving.

God has charged me with a vision to seek 20 women who have experienced adversity and are not simply surviving but THRIVING! We often observe women we may consider thriving and not know their back story. The purpose and heart of this book anthology project are to inspire hope through the stories that these not 20 but 22 courageous Queens Who Defied the Odds bounced back from despite the challenges they have faced. Each of their stories of adversity, triumph, and victory will restore hope and transform lives. "Do not throw away this confident trust in the Lord. Remember the great reward it brings you! Patient endurance is what you need now so that you will continue to do God's will. Then you will receive all that he has promised." Hebrews 10:35–36, NLT

God indeed has a plan. Rise up, my Sisters! In preparation for a powerful read, get in your comfy chair with a glass of water and tissues. Each story will encourage and give you a glimpse of why you had to go through what you went through. It's a part of YOUR assignment!

Empowered to Inspire YOU!

Cheryl

Trina Fitzgerald currently resides in Pennsylvania with her husband, where they have raised a charming young daughter who is filled with compassion. Upon graduation from Philadelphia, Pa. school system, she felt led to earn her degree in the Hospitality Industry where she could actively utilize her talent and skills to provide comfort and care in an industry that requires her unique skills.

In order to be more effective as a leader she went on to earn her degree in leadership through the Harcum College Leadership program, which has taught her how to be more effective in the Insurance Industry where she has been employed for over 25 years. Her attention to detail and changes are forever affecting how we provide service to customers. Because of her value, worth and knowledge, she sits on the Board of He Covered Me Inc., which is a non-profit organization that provides support to young adults who are aging out of the foster care system and lack any familial support. Her compassion and empathy for supporting young adults has made her a vital part of the organization.

Who Am I That Nothing Should Ever Happen To Me?

TRINA FITZGERALD

It was the summer I was planning my September wedding when the entire left side of my body was numb from head to toe—even my face, including my tongue, lips, and teeth. I know it sounds crazy, but even my lady parts were numb. The summer of 2000 was the first sign that something was definitely wrong with me. I'm the kind of person who always thinks it is going to get better, no need to go to the doctor right away. No need to pay the co-pay; nothing has fallen off my body yet. I thought it was stress related and it would eventually go away after my wedding—and it did. Now, of course, looking back I know more than ever the effects stress can have on the body. Unfortunately, I also knew my mother was not excited about my upcoming nuptials. Needless to say, it was an extremely stressful time in my life.

Fast forward six years and add a baby girl into the equation. That's when I woke up at the end of 2006 on a sunny Sunday morning with partial vision in my right eye. I remember clearly, no pun intended, I kept thinking this must be the result of cleaning fluid I used the day before when I was doing housework. I washed my eyes out repeatedly with cold water and then Visine, but nothing worked. It was like having a frosted shade pulled down over your eye or a bad seat at your favorite theater and there is a pillar obstructing your view of the stage. You can't see around it or through it. This went on for months because admittedly, I can be extremely stubborn plus cheap since I didn't want to pay the co-payment at the doctor's office. I naively thought my eyesight would return as quickly as I had lost it.

It would be months before I finally went to the doctor. As a matter of fact, I started out at the optometrist's office first because I already had my annual physical, so I knew it was not diabetes. Besides, I had been working out on a regular basis, drinking only the highest quality bottled water, and my diet consisted of salads and nuts. The optometrist did every eye test that she could think of but was completely baffled as to the cause of my vision loss. In addition to my vision issues, I was experiencing numbness in my left leg and foot. Six-inch heels were out of the question. I would not be wearing those anytime soon, which really sucked because I loved wearing a good pair of high heels, I remember my family and I were out to dinner on one of those hot summer Philly nights and I had on flip-flops. I went to take my young daughter to the bathroom when I heard my husband yelling across the restaurant, "You forgot your shoe!" I looked down and sure enough I only had one shoe on. I could not feel a thing. I started to notice other symptoms like losing my balance or bumping into things all the time. It became so bad I started telling my husband when I bumped into something, just in case I had a bruise later and couldn't remember when or how it happened. He would remind me I walked into the shelf at Wawa's. My response would be, "That's right, I did." Meanwhile my body looked like that board game 'Connect the Dots' from all the bruises and bumps on it.

While I lived in Pennsylvania, I worked in Delaware and my daughter attended school there as well. So every morning, as we did so many times before going to work and school, I now really needed her since my eyes became so sensitive to natural sunlight or clouds. Deciphering what color the traffic lights were had become a serious problem for me. My baby would shout out the color of the lights to me. "Red light, Mommy; green light, Mommy go!" And off I would go. When I finally arrived in the office, it would take almost 45 minutes for my eyes to adjust. Many times, I would sit at my desk with my eyes closed, waiting for my vision to return to its new normal, blurred. Thankfully the IT person was able to increase the fonts on my desktop so I could see without having to sit up so close to my computer.

Coworkers started calling me little Ray-Ray for Ray Charles, of course, since the movie was out at the time. So it was funny, and I tried to maintain a sense of humor, although I was becoming frustrated with the lack of information I was receiving from the doctor's office. One of my family members accused me of making it up for attention. Yes, I would claim I could not see for attention, sure. That's what I wanted to say, but it wasn't worth the argument. Besides, I had already made up my mind no matter what the outcome, I was going to go through it with a good attitude, considering someone could have it a lot worse than me.

Then there was the ghetto eye test. You know, when you cover one eye and check your eyesight, then switch your hand and check your other eye. This went on for the entire ordeal. Every time I had an appointment, I would pray that they would not take my license. If truth be told I always got the first letter correct on the eye chart because everyone knows that "E" is the first letter of the eye chart but after that I did not have a clue what the next letter was. Truthfully, not being able to drive was not an option for me.

Meantime, I started a year and a half long relationship with so many doctors I lost count. Some I never received results from or heard from again. I remember one doctor took over 100 pictures of my eyes blinking after he injected dye into my arm.

There were many days I would have to do everything in reverse at a moment's notice if I received a call from a doctor who could fit me in their schedule that day. First, I would ask my boss if I could leave early; thank goodness my bosses were very understanding. I also never missed a day of work because of the situation. It was important for me to go to work every day that I could in case it was something serious that might have required me to take months off at a time. Plus going to work every day made me feel like I was maintaining some sort of normalcy in my life. Once everything was cleared with my bosses, I would have to pick my daughter up early from school, get on the expressway and rush to downtown Philadelphia to take an even weirder eye test than the last one. I was beginning to feel like a human guinea pig. I started to feel like the doctors didn't want to diagnose me for fear of lawsuits in case their diagnosis was incorrect.

This mystery illness was slowly turning into a nightmare. I would talk about it to anybody who would listen to me. All you had to do was say hello to me and you would know my entire story of what had transpired for the past year of my life. The funny thing is my mother would always say, "Don't tell people your business." Guess what? I was becoming desperate for answers and did not care who knew what was happening to me. I needed an answer. I wanted to return to my normal lifestyle as soon as possible.

Amid everything going on with my physical body, the loss of vision, the numbness I was experiencing, I would continue to thank God and tell myself who am I that nothing should ever happen to me.

I would keep a positive attitude and a sense of humor, which really helped me deal with the circumstances and go about life as normally as possible.

Fortunately, one afternoon a VP in my office named Kevin, a very nice older gentleman who didn't come into our office very often, so he was completely unaware of what I was experiencing with my eyesight, asked me to come to his office to assist with something on his computer. Kevin was probably the only person in the building who hadn't heard my story. I remember telling him I couldn't see the screen. He would have to make it bigger if he wanted my help. Sure enough, he asked me what was going on and naturally I had no problem sharing my story. I had it down-pat, with jokes and all. But what I did not expect was him to give me the name of an eye doctor and tell them that he referred me. By this time, I was so jaded with people giving me numbers and their diagnosis based on their cousin's or auntie's condition I thought, *Sure, I will give them a call tomorrow.* Guess what? I did. At this point I had nothing to lose. I called the next morning and surprisingly, the doctor's office was located at a hospital five minutes from my home. I was able to get an appointment with the doctor for the following week. I must admit I went to this appointment not expecting much aside from just handing over another $40.00 co-pay for no answers again. However, this time was different: For one, the doctor was young, and second, he looked into my eyes and said, "I love you" (no, no, he didn't say that). He said, "I think I know what the problem is. You need to make an appointment with the doctor downstairs who specializes in this issue."

Obviously, I said. "What issue?" Not surprisingly, the doctor responded, "I can't tell you yet; the doctor will have to see you first and confirm my suspicion."

Okay, I made the appointment with the doctor he recommended I see for the following week—another $40.00 bucks. This doctor was a Neuro-Ophthalmologist and yes, he also looked into my eyes, but this time he said, "I'm pretty sure I know what it is. I need you to get an MRI to confirm what I think it is."

Now I had never had this test before, but I had heard of it, so I was a little skeptical about being enclosed in this tube-like structure. Plus, how big is this machine? Will I fit?

I was able to get an appointment that week for the MRI at 6:30 in the morning. No problem, I can do that so long as a diagnosis is closer. The morning came for the MRI. I was ready to take this test, but nobody told me how loud it was or that they would be injecting dye into me halfway through the test. I felt like a turkey at Thanksgiving, being basted and shoved back into the oven for more baking. They also put this helmet on my head with a mirror attached so I could watch me lie still watching me.

Finally, after a year and a half of countless doctor's visits, I received a diagnosis from the nurse that my doctor sent to my house with all this hospital equipment. Well, sort of a diagnosis; he said, "Do you have MS?" I said, "NO!" He said, "Are you sure? Because this is what I normally do for my MS patients." Once again, I said, "NO, I do not have MS." I felt like saying, "Do you hear the words that are coming out of my mouth? NO, I do not have MS."

Well, regardless if I had it or not, he was sent to show me how to administer steroids intravenously for the next week. The nurse proceeded to put a needle in my arm that would stay in for the entire week, which meant I had to wear it to work every day. I had to get up two hours early to fix the drip and start the process of taking steroids that would help me regain my vision. Frankly, I would have done whatever I had to do to get my vision back so I could see my family and not lose my independence.

A week later after the nurse's visit, I was able to see my doctor, who I trusted had all the answers to the puzzle regarding this year and a half of searching for answers. He said, "You have a little MS" and I replied, "Is that like being a little pregnant?" I didn't know so I had to ask. The perplexing matter to me was I didn't start crying or get upset. I immediately thought, "Am I going to be in a wheelchair for the rest of my life?" All I could think of was the comedian Richard Pryor or Annette Funicello from the Mickey Mouse show. They both had MS and were both in wheelchairs. I asked the doctor if that would be my fate in life because I didn't have time for that. Everything I knew about MS, which wasn't much, ultimately led to being permanently wheelchair-bound, depending on other people to take care of you. The doctor assured me that would not be the case at all, that the advancements that had been made over the past 20 years or so helped people live a productive, normal life. Regardless of what the doctor said, I felt complete relief because at least now I knew what I was dealing with. It is the uncertainty that can drive you crazy if you let it.

I remember going home after the visit and my sister was staying with us at the time, so I told her that I had relapsing MS. She immediately started to cry. I told her, "I'm not dying. I will take the medicine, and everything will be okay." I phoned my husband at work and he was extremely supportive, asking what he could do to help me. My reply was, "Really, nothing. I will take the medicine and go to my doctor's appointments and everything will be fine."

Now I mentioned that I took the steroids from the doctor, but what I didn't say was I took them at the end of April. However, I didn't regain my eyesight until September. It happened so gradually over the summer I don't remember exactly when it returned fully. I just know it returned and I was grateful for that. After about two years I had a relapse, but this time it was in my back so my doctor switched me to a pill that other patients who had MS were using and doing well on with little to no side effects. The thing about MS is while there is no cure for it, they can slow down the progression of the disease and most people can live a normal life.

I thought it was interesting that after being diagnosed with MS, when I would share with people what I had they would tell me I didn't look like I had it. In many instances people would share with me about their loved ones who had MS and were not doing well. The theme seemed to be that they were not taking their medicine because they were waiting to be healed by God. I totally get that, but I believe God made scientists to discover medicine that can help people live a better life while waiting for a healing from God. Therefore, I decided to eat my medicine like M&M's until I am healed, and I do believe I will be healed from this hideous disease.

I have lived with this disease for the past 13 years and I could tell you story after story about my journey but the truth is, I am so very grateful. If I have to have something—and we all will face some trials in our lives—I'm grateful that it came at a time when the advancements in treating this disease have allowed me not to be wheelchair-bound. I may not be able to strut in high heels anymore but I'm grateful there is an assortment of flats that are colorful and stylish. I'm grateful to see my family every day. I certainly don't take that lightly. God has allowed me to still work after all these years with no problem. God is so awesome. I don't have to pay for my medicine. I'm still driving!!! The list goes on and on. I not only survived but I'm definitely thriving, living my best life.

Last, I would like to leave you with a thought: Who are you that nothing should ever happen to you? And when it does—and it will—how will you handle it?

Ruby Echols was born in upstate New York and raised in Philadelphia. She relocated back to Philadelphia from previously teaching Middle school students in Atlanta, Georgia. She was a Special Education teacher for ten years. Ruby has worn many hats within the education arena for over fifteen years. Her specialty was Language Arts and Reading. Prior to teaching she worked for the United States Postal Service.

Ruby attended Florida A&M University and Temple University. She is pursuing additional studies at the graduate level. She has taught pre-school students in her earlier years and children with special needs. She was also a tutor in an after-school program and the facilitator for a Girl's Club at the Middle school level. She has been blessed to have had the opportunity to travel abroad within six countries, such as Germany, Netherlands, France, UK, Belgium and Switzerland. She traveled with students who were able to delegate and focus on leadership, community involvement and personal development, while having fun and experiencing other cultures. Traveling is a hobby and Ruby is also pursuing her love of writing.

Providing children with a foundation of God in their lives, coupled with a loving, developmental sound foundation for learning, is an ongoing passion. Ruby strives to create and maintain an environment where children can grow and thrive, while exploring the world around them. Her demeanor has always been one of caring for her fellow man. She stands on and holds a strong conviction that it does take a village to raise a child.

All My Life...

RUBY ECHOLS

Trials and tribulations will always show up during one's lifetime. We must minimize the downs and establish a permanent basis for success. One has to wonder and contemplate if one's journey has circled to completion during one's lifespan. When I was a young girl growing up, mortality never entered my world. Nowadays, as I leave middle age and enter into another stage of life, it has become the norm and death resurfaces continuously. I can say that I came from a privileged background and in the twinkling of an eye, all which was, ceased to exist. I came from a two-family household and a middle-class neighborhood. My family was one of the first to own a color television, and while growing up we owned a pet monkey. Yes, a monkey, which we had for more than five years. All my life I enjoyed having family around. Then, poof this all was gone in the twinkling of an eye. I was the apple of my parents' eyes and was the baby girl. This was my namesake before it became fashionable in the new age.

Grandparents and the elderly should be cherished because they are our walking archives. I would listen endlessly, to my great-aunt and uncle and they would tell me stories about my mother and her siblings and how they grew up in Wakulla Springs, near Tallahassee, Florida. My great-grandfather owned a general store and my great-great grandfather was one of the first Black principals in the state of Florida. We had good roots. Many Blacks migrated from the South to Northern states in which they felt were better opportunities; millions were a part of this movement. All my life I have wanted to know my family roots and learned from the elders in the family about the slave, which was my great-great grandfather, meeting the Seminole Indian along the shores of South Carolina, and thus my genealogy began.

It is sad to say and remember that even though I and my siblings came from a good family, there was a lot of dysfunction. Yet these good multitudes of relatives were not available when they were needed for seven parentless young children. No one stepped up to the plate and took the newly-made orphans in. The older generation of my family allowed my oldest brother to state that my mother told him on her deathbed to not separate us, and he lied to the elders that this was her dying wish. So the well-to-do elders from various cities like Cincinnati, Tallahassee and Philadelphia allowed a 21-year-old young black man fresh out of jail the responsibility of raising seven siblings, ranging from two to 12. It was later learned that the older brother also had a deep heroin addiction. So you can do the math of the detrimental effect this had on all the children involved. This was a problematic issue stemming from this separation of siblings that still lingers to this day. Dysfunction is a common denominator till this very day because of the upbringing, raising or lack thereof that transcends currently as well. I lost a brother four years ago who had overcome the dilemma of losing our parents to become a star basketball player and later dealt as a drug dealer. My brother would then serve time as he learned his lesson and became an upstanding pillar in the community. But due to loving and marrying the wrong women, it cost him his life, and this was such a hard, wrenching facet in the entire siblings' lives. It still lingers to this very day. It was such a mind-blowing event that probably could or may have been avoided with the right people or choices in his life. One utterance or call for our father, Lord God, before dying shall save your soul. I know and believe my brother to know this. We need to break this chain in my family. To this very day there are some family members who only talk with certain members and so forth. When does the madness stop? We are here on this side for such a short time and we need to be better at being good to one another. I lost a sister this year and for reasons I honestly do not know, the siblings were not informed by her children of her passing. But God is oh so gracious, he allowed us to share great moments together just two months before her transition. We laughed, prayed, talked and shared stories. Dear Lord, I am so thankful.

Growing up in Upstate New York and losing both parents at a very young age, I barely escaped the ramifications and horrors of foster care. It was arranged for me to relocate with an older sibling who was newly married with children. This sister, who raised me like her very own, is the one I lost this very year. Upon moving to Philadelphia at age 13, I experienced a culture shock. I hadn't gone to school with other Blacks before and it just felt different. Yes, Blacks experience this too. I had to learn to integrate myself among my own kind. I always thought at that time that my sister was so much older but as we grew older, I learned it was only a six-year difference. I felt a special closeness and bond to my mother/sister. It was offered and available to me to live with one of my Caucasian teachers who adored and felt compassionate to step in and help me out. There was a teacher who took me under his care and saw that I attended the best of schools and monitored my progress until I left the area. My teacher saw no color and we crossed the color barrier long before people made headlines about integration of fair public education. The teachers knew my plight and wanted to facilitate the arduous task of me being taken care of. My extreme intellectual prowess at such an early age gave me the upper hand in allowing opportunities to manifest for me. One has to wonder if I was just an average student if this would have come to fruition. I felt appreciative that someone would want to do this for me, but I declined and relocated with my sister. We had an aunt who also lived in Philadelphia, who helped when she saw fit.

Along the way, I was destined to meet a family in Philadelphia that took me in as their own and we've been together as family for more than fifty years. There's family that's not blood and there's blood that's not family. I know there are people that can identify with this. All my life this mantra of events seems to dominate. During my childhood, after I relocated, I was nearly a victim of molestation from a family member whom I trusted. If not for my quick thinking and ability to ward off this much older stronger individual I would have been another statistic. It shames me to state that I told members of my family who needed to know and yet the person was able to continue to be around other young children and he stayed within the family, but I always kept one eye open at all times around that snake. Quite depressing to learn there are a large percentage of victims who never come forth, afraid of shame and adverse reaction from what people would think. All my life, I have been fighting and warding off demons.

During the 60s race was what was shaping the nation. Blacks were under great turmoil in becoming citizens and getting acceptance on many levels. African Americans were being denied access to good housing, high quality education, employment, and just literally basic amenities. Many were exposed to blatant racism throughout their employment and literally all facets of everyday life. I can remember in middle school leaving school to go downtown to the school board to insist on equal rights for the students. I went with a friend and even though this did not affect me personally, I was still willing to be a participant for the cause. I was already going to a predominantly white school due to my high score placement. Yet I wanted to be a part of the struggle and happen to make it on the evening news. I guess participating in protests and helping others has been in my DNA for a long time. This struggle continues today as I have become an advocate for social injustice and belong to numerous organizations that fight for voting rights and equal rights for all.

Blatant racism has reared its ugly head throughout my life from time to time. I can remember working for a government entity where I was a victim of racial and sexual discrimination and harassment. There were times when I was approached or asked if I needed anything or called to the office just to sit and chat. It was at these times I was given the opportunity to say what I needed or wanted and could have had. There was room for great advancement, better hours, and all of this, if I was willing to have a date. Yes, I turned it down, and then I was blackballed. Yes, there were some women who took the bait for advancement and couldn't look me in the eyes when we were in passing because they knew I knew what they accepted. Please believe a person, if they say a company or boss doesn't or does like you. Once I did not return the favor, I was singled out. Believe me, it happens.

This federal entity was a very lucrative position and many people have retired nicely from this opportunity. It was a place where a basic and minimal education allowed you to advance and earn a very nice wage. Many individuals had a nice income and were able to obtain many material possessions, send children to college, pay for homes and live a good life. This is where and how I acquired my possession and love of cocaine. You see, curiosity can kill the cat. I was reeled in by seeking. Thank God it was short-lived. I could say I was a functional addict. I went to work most times and earned my pay, only to spend an astronomical amount on this popular drug of choice during the epidemic. Many times I didn't have to pay anything, though; I just had to be in the company of others who were willing to share. As one very popular famous musical star stated, she only free-based, and that crack was whack. It still fit the bill of being a very addictive, crushing drug. Though I wasn't addicted to crack I can still state that it was only through the grace of God that it did not manifest into something bigger than life. I can remember the agony of longing for this fix and through prayer and determination and because I then had a son who depended on me, I just quit, cold turkey. All my life temptations are all around, but God delivers all who seek his hand in deliverance.

God heard my pleas and delivered me. I know it was only through the grace of God. I decided to leave this occupation for other opportunities, which were already in the plan before the onset of this distorted representation of what good times looked like.

Of course, once you have acquired being the Queen, you seek out your King. My life choices of men have not always been pretty. I can remember growing up and being the apple of many eyes. I was the Nia in the neighborhood. At least that's what I've heard and been told. Though I went off to college at 16, I returned to Philadelphia after two and a half years and started working. I worked for great enterprises. During this time, I met many knuckleheads and desirables along the way. I also met the love of my life, twice. If I could do things differently, of course I would. I would forgive my fiancé for stepping out on me. A high majority of women are still with their mate because they forgave them. I understand this better now. At first, I would think that the women were weak or desperate. Ladies, if it is a good man, I think forgiveness is in order. I let a great provider slip through my hands. It was not because of the material things that he gave me but because he was a genuine, decent person. I must admit that I was negligent in not giving him the attention and affection that he needed, and so he went looking. We all learn from our mistakes. If I could do it all over, there are so many things that I would change. He was a keeper. I must admit I've had some great providers and I was a kept woman. But where is the love? I began to look in the wrong places. I also met some losers. Then there were the ones I thought would change, or that I could change them. Or that it would be different this time. No, not yet, it's going to get better and better never comes along. I was constantly told how good I looked or how spectacular I was about this or that and yet, marriage never came. I'm not saying that marriage defines a woman or that it is significant in determining a woman's worth.

So where is my significant other? I've had two engagements, and one secret wedding. I never told anyone of the marriage because it was going to be revealed at a later time. I just didn't want to live in sin, so we married and decided we would tell everyone when we finished planning the nuptials. It lasted until the seven-year itch, and poof, he was gone. I wonder long and hard sometimes, did I give up too easily again? All my life quick decisions became unwise ones.

The older a woman becomes the more the chances of finding a significant other drastically decrease. This doesn't allow us the understanding or desire to suggest that we must settle. Settling is not an option. During these times we live much longer and what is yours is yours. There are some people who like the idea of living their lives in solitude or single. This ideology suits them just fine. This institution of life is fine for those who find it pleasurable and suitable to their needs and wants. The institution of marriage is not for everyone. What is for me will be mine.

Through this all, I am grateful for the exposure and learning about God early in life. I was raised in the church and have always had the understanding about the power of God. There were moments in time that I did not lean or wait on the Lord. I feel as though these are the times that I failed miserably. One has to believe and hold steadfast in the truth that you will be delivered. It is through these trying times that I have been able to sustain and pull through it all, through the grace of GOD.

In just the past ten months alone, I have endured a few medical situations. I was diagnosed with a pulmonary embolism in both lungs at the beginning of the year, and then Covid. Health officials and the world have learned and been affected by this worldwide epidemic. Many families have lost or had the dilemma of caring for relatives affected by this crippling pandemic. Then there's need to make the complicated decision of whether to have this newly-developed vaccine or not. It is primarily a matter of choice among the public. The decision to vaccinate is determined by each individual. I feel as though it is not a decision to be made for the masses.

During my hospital stay I began to hear a ringing sound in my ears and it was determined to be tinnitus. It is a condition with no or little public awareness, one that leaves its victims with little support and fewer options. Tinnitus is a crippling, annoying condition. There are many people who are not aware of this and there are few studies or help to determine and treat tinnitus. It is debilitating and not much can be done about it. It could come from medicine side effects or hearing loss. Many physicians offer minimal help. This condition has caused me many sleepless nights and has taken a toll on my quality of life. I have had to relocate to be with family members so that I could have people around the clock or in attendance. Yet I have learned that this is not feasible because everyone has a life and though the heart is in it to help, it comes with a price. It is not like it was when I was growing up. Family matters. There is just so much to do and so little time. I have always been an independent person and now I have to depend on others.

I am not crippled but I am at the mercy of sound. There are days I do not want to get out of bed or fight another day. Each day comes with the assumption that it could be a hollowing day. Each day I seek out God's blessing and guidance in carrying me through another adversity. I definitely do not want to become a burden and I want to be able to be self-sufficient. I know God only gives us what we can endure and there is hope and belief that this too shall pass. There are some days that I don't know how to get through the day, and then there are good days. The underlying difficulty in it all is that no physician or specialist can really say where it is stemming from and that is what becomes so depressing, the uncertainty. All my life trials and tribulations only make me stronger in leaning on God's ever-changing hand through it all.

All my life I have had struggles and challenges and yet somehow, I have always managed to come through. I always say to the many from the outside looking in, life is not always what it may seem. There are people who seem like they have it made or have it all together but who may have the same struggles as you. I was the girl who had it all and yet, at various times throughout my life, I struggled through many growing pains. There was the loss of a loved one, the loss of a job, the loss of items, and the loss and humility of losing it all. I have had to start all over from the bottom up. I started from scratch in a new town, taking instructions and orders from someone I knew was less competent than me, but there wasn't anything I could do but suck it up. We are all human and it's all right because it's going to work out, because even though in my life, I am going through trials, I believe and know God's got me.

Sheila Bell-Thomas was born in Manhattan, New York, raised by relatives in Philadelphia, Pa. She attended catholic school from first to twelfth grade, graduated from Penn State University and pursued a master's degree at St. Joseph's University. She moved to Michigan where she stayed for eight years then came back to Philadelphia, Pa.

Sheila came to salvation late in life, but found out no matter how late it may have seemed, her life was still full of purpose and meaning. Whatever her situation may have been, she was given the authority to touch a heart and save a soul.

In 2008, Sheila was called and licensed as Minister. She was ordained-licensed as a Pastor in October 2016 and consecrated in January 2021 through the Kingdom of God Is At Hand (KOGIAH), International Healing Ministries where the visionary is Dr. Donna Jeanne Christopher. She is also privileged to be a facilitator at her school, Tree of Life Institute of Biblical Studies.

Sheila is a published author of three books, Fountain of Grace, Droplets of Grace and 365 Days of Grace in His Sight. Proclaiming God's grace has consistently helped her to understand. She was also encouraged by the fact that grace goes beyond style, poise and charm. She's found that grace is more than a prayer over food or being given extra time when running late. Grace goes beyond man's thoughts, and abilities and does not have its boundaries rooted in what the world mandates. Grace offers freedom from bondage to those who live life under the "Fountains of Grace".

Abandoned? Not Me!

SHEILA BELL-THOMAS

My mother, Lottie Zell, gave birth to me in Manhattan, New York in 1956. She died from an illegal abortion when I was fourteen months old. However, before my mother died, she went to Philadelphia, PA, to ask her sister, Christine, to take care of me until she returned. Being close sisters as they were, they always came to each other's aid. One thing I do remember at fourteen months was Lottie saying over and over again, "I'll be back" as she opened the door to leave for what would be the last time. I actually knew what that meant and I never forgot. I will explain further in the story.

I found out later the adults had decided it was best for me not to attend my mother's funeral. I believe they knew how close we were and did not want to traumatize me any further. For example, my husband and I had taken our youngest daughter, who was less than six months old at the time, to her first funeral. After we sat down, she began to cry and scream hysterically, to the point I had to take her out of the room. After she calmed down, I tried it again and the same thing happened. I mentioned this scenario to give credence to the fact that while babies may not be able to speak yet, they are keenly aware of what they feel and acutely sensitive to what they hear.

Another validation was made on Sunday, June 20, 2021 when I watched Dr. Charles Stanley. He was talking about his father, who died when he was nine months old. One of the members of the church came to see him with her daughter, who was also nine months old. She reached out for him to take her from her mother's arms and he did. This is a perfect example of love and bonding taking place when you least expect it. She is in college now and they have a growing relationship to this very day.

My aunt Christine shared with me how she found out my mother had passed. She told me she was lying across her bed resting when suddenly she felt a quick tug on her leg. She shook her leg as if to shake the tug away. Still not knowing what it was, she laid her head back down to continue to rest. A few minutes later, she felt a tug on her leg again and at the same time the phone rang. It was her other sister on the phone, Aunt Thelma, who lived in Harlem, New York at the time. She had called Aunt Christine to let her know that Lottie Zell had just died. Immediately Aunt Christine concluded that the tug on her leg was my mother. Aunt Christine shared what happened with her sister, Thelma, and they both came to the same conclusion that it was Lottie Zell.

Aunt Thelma's recollection of the story went like this. She was aware Lottie Zell came back to New York with the intention to end the pregnancy, and she knew the method was not safe—illegal, even. However, during that time, there were several "secret places" where people would go to get these procedures done. The places were not the most sanitary but were accepted because they were affordable. Once the process was completed, they called the number Lottie Zell had given them as the emergency contact person, who was Aunt Thelma. They gave her the address where she could find my mother and gave themselves enough time to leave before Aunt Thelma got there. She arrived at "the secret place" to find Lottie Zell lying down. She must have been so happy to see her sister as she walked into "the secret place." She said to Thelma, "If you don't get me some water, I'm going to die." You see, unbeknownst to her, she was hemorrhaging and she was extremely thirsty as a result. Thelma went to get her some water and when she returned, she gave her the water, and those were Lottie Zell's last words.

For several nights after the funeral, Aunt Christine told me I was crying in my crib and she heard me yelling repeatedly, "Leave me alone!" Aunt Christine would come in and console me as best she could. Apparently, it happened often enough to cause Aunt Christine to have a brief talk with my deceased mother. She said, "Lottie Zell, I will take care of Sheila as best I can" and "You do not have to come back." And she never came back.

I remember a time which occurred between the ages of two and three, when I was still anticipating my mother's return. Whenever I heard the doorbell ring, I would run to the door in hopes that it would be my mother coming to get me. This happened so many times that one day when the doorbell rang, I heard my aunt's friend, who was visiting that day, ask her, "When are you going to tell her?" I actually heard and understood what she said and it stopped me in my tracks. But having been brought up during a time when a child was seen and not heard, I said nothing. Obviously, it was difficult for my aunt Christine to tell me my mother was not coming back. I do not remember exactly how or precisely when she told me, but I was told.

I came to realize that I was abandoned by several people in my life. It began with my mother, Lottie Zell, my father James, my aunt Christine and other relatives. I understood then that you can live with people and still feel the effects of what it is like to be abandoned. According to the Merriam-Webster Dictionary, to be abandoned means "to leave and never return to (someone who needs protection or help)." It was not until I wrote this chapter that I had the mind to address the root of my bondage. This definition described how I felt as a child but the dilemma was, I could not explain it. I did not have the words to describe what I was experiencing as a fourteen-month-old.

It was clearly impossible for a fourteen-month-old to describe, let alone understand, what just happened. The word that comes to mind that best describes my confusion was abandonment. One may never equate abandonment with not receiving words of affirmation, not experiencing actions such as a warm embrace or a gentle kiss, not being told you are loved or not hearing how appreciated you are. I called these "simple acts of abandonment, or SAA." SAAs can begin at a young age like it had for me and if not resolved, it can have life-long effects. This abandonment issue has been brewing in me all of my life as an unexplained void that was not filled and resulted in the creation of a suppressed hiding place.

The interesting difference for me was realizing none of the simple acts of abandonment were done on purpose. It was not my fault and it was not my choice. Lottie Zell made the decision for my life and I was not aware of what details involved. Aunt Christine accepted the responsibility for raising me. I was not left on a church step, sold on the black market, dropped off at a hospital, or placed in an orphanage. I was destined to live with relatives who took good care of me but did not realize they were operating in SAA. I did not know and neither did they.

They did what they thought was necessary for my growth and development. I will never take that away from them. However, I know this relationship is something only my birth-giver can give me for sure. I know now because this was the piece of my life that was missing. As a child, I could not bring understanding to this emptiness I experienced. Today, I can describe my experience with SAA by the consistent aloneness I felt, even when in the presence of my new family. They could not replace what I was missing. I forgive them for not knowing.

The brief fourteen months of my parents knowing me and me knowing them was the essence of what I miss, and I forgive both parents for this. I was abandoned, left to my own plans, but who has plans at fourteen months of age? There was no compass or map to give me direction, to help me navigate this heavy emptiness. I had no choice but to live with my situation silently, not knowing who would rescue me from this desolation. How could I explain something like this as a child when all of this was new to me as well? Who would be sensitive enough to know I was experiencing something like this at such a young age?

There is a delicate balance that results from this, I know. If I were to describe this feeling in more detail, I would say I was the one who felt the difference, the void, the most. And because I did not know how to express to my new family what I felt was missing, the confusion in my feelings only festered. I cannot blame my relatives for not knowing what I was used to with my birth-giver, but I do know there was a vacancy.

Yes, I felt abandoned, having missed out on the love and affection I knew I had briefly experienced from both parents. You may ask, what about my father? I loved my father dearly and while he wanted to take me, Aunt Christine wanted to honor Lottie Zell's request when she dropped me off that final day. All of this was taken away as a result of the sudden death of my mother. Now I was placed in a situation where I had to live with relatives I barely knew. For all I know, they probably felt the same way about me, confused as to what steps to take next.

I cannot express how appreciative and grateful I am for my aunt Christine to follow through on my mother's wish. Nonetheless, it was hard for me and for that matter it can be hard for anyone at such a young age to experience something as tragic as this. What was I to do? How was I to know how to blend in with my new family? I did not know how.

Aunt Christine had a daughter the same age as me but her approach toward raising me was more neutral. There was still a major void left in me which included my search for the love that I remembered having my first fourteen months. I wanted it from the family, who was not aware of how to share that love, which caused me to sink deeper into myself.

At this point, I understand there are many different family dynamics but at that time, I did not know how to make "it" make sense when I did not know what "it" was. I knew there was a gap but I did not know how to express the gap or how the gap was affecting me. However, what I have learned was each family creates, grooms, nurtures and becomes accustomed to their own family lifestyle and how they show love, a feeling of security, and what it means to be a vital part of the family unit. And it begins with the family members knowing what is valuable in the formation of the family nucleus. This nucleic component is what validates the DNA of each family member with a sense of belonging; otherwise, you feel like a fish out of water. In essence, having observed my new family and how they functioned and interacted with one another has shed a bright light in my dark place. It was plain for me to see that I needed more than they realized but it was not their fault. How does a fourteen-month-old talk about what they are feeling? How does a fourteen-month-old close the gap that was created? The answer is, they don't!

I saw my new family unfold and blossom before my eyes but I did not know how to be a part of it. Being a part of a blended family can be very complex, especially if you cannot put your finger on what the complexity is that needs to be addressed. Every family unit operates differently and according to what they value the most. When it comes to a blended family, the hope is that each individual will be given attention on what makes them unique and special and there will be a focus on incorporating those differences as a positive entity for the family. While this is the hope, focusing on the development of an individual is not always achieved when abandonment is the hidden issue.

For the longest time and until now, I have experienced varying degrees of hopelessness and confusion, not being able to comprehend what I was suffering from. I am sure that the day and time this was happening to me, it did not become a red flag for my family; after all, my basic needs were being met. However, what they did not see were the increasing levels of my depression as a result of trying to deal with it the best way I knew how. The abandonment was what perpetuated the depression daily, and I could not forget or let go of what little bit of the past comforted me.

What I think might have helped over time was sharing with me the details of who Lottie Zell was during her 38 years of life. I would have loved to hear the stories about her dreams and desires, her character, and her quirks. I do know she was a good cook and awesome baker. I have asked questions about her and will continue to ask questions of those who have been fortunate enough to have been in her presence. Until then, my suggestion for the future of blended families of all kinds is to discuss these hidden issues that families tend to not talk about or at best, consult a professional, godly counsel who can explore the root problems that plague the family. The issues are there.

In fact, other disparities will be uncovered and addressed because they are of grave concern for the stability of family continuity.

As a child and through my teenage years, there were many factors that contributed to who I was. For example, over the years my desires were: I wanted to take singing classes, dance lessons, and pursue my interest in art. I even took the art test found in the back of a magazine insert where you had to draw a baby deer, mail it in and the school would contact you and they did. However, because the response to each request was not favorable, I drew even more into myself because I felt I did not know what path to take. You see, while it is ok to say, "This is wrong for you," it is equally important to say, and for the child to hear, "This may be right for you." There must be a balance. I know it may be hard at times, but it is the parent or guardian's responsibility to train a child in the way they should go or guide them into the greatness their gifts will allow them to be.

One incident in my life I am not so proud of but I have gotten over it. I am willing to share only because this was a pivotal time in my life where I needed help and got it. It was a classic case of looking for love in all the wrong places. I went to a club one evening and a guy came up to me at the bar. We talked for a while and I left. I went out with him again only to find out he was a pimp but for some reason, that did not bother me at all. I guess it was the attention I was given. We went out again and I sensed he was trying to groom me for the "profession." I went to work the next day, which was going to be my last day. When the work day was over, I walked out of the building, and to my surprise, my sister and cousin were outside saying, "Sheila, what are you doing?" That was the right question. Without answering, I looked past them to the parked cars, and there he was waiting for me to come to the car—but I did not. While I was looking at him, I was being smothered with hugs and love. When I arrived home, my aunt Christine told me she was going to dress up like a lady of the night and go looking for me if I did not come home. While it was a serious life lesson for me, we had a good laugh about the whole thing and I never felt more loved than on that day. Keep in mind, many unforeseen circumstances can cause an unexpected turn in life, as in my case.

My breakthrough occurred when I went to a Birthing/Deliverance conference in May 2021. I became acquainted with a person who has a mothering spirit and she listened to me. After I shared my story, she embraced me like a mother would and spoke as if she were my mother asking for forgiveness. Like the tears that fell down my face, the resentment and disappointment had waned and the heaviness was lifted.

No matter what it looked like in the past, there is always the hope for things to get better. Rest assured, most things we encounter are working together for our benefit in the end. It may not feel like it while we are going "through" the situation. I leave you with these words of wisdom the Holy Spirit gave me. We will be met with two words in our lifetime, which are found in the word "through," and they are "rough" and "tough." These wonder twins, like grace and mercy, teach us many lessons, some of which we would rather avoid but are necessary to experience. Their purpose is to mold and shape us into the vessels of honor we are intended to be. But my, my, my, once we make it to the place called "through," we can exhale and enjoy the fruit of that knowledge. Once we reach the other side of "through," we become stronger, possessing the power to make it "through" to the next challenge, knowing with each challenge, in the end, the outcome will be in our favor.

Robin M. Shine Maddox is a native Philadelphian born to Rev. Dr. Robert P. and Barbara Shine. She is the eldest of four children.

For over the past thirty years, Robin's professional and rewarding career track landed her opportunities to work in the private, non-profit and government sectors. Since 2008, she continues to serve as Constituent Service Representative for Pennsylvania State Senator Vincent Hughes.

In addition to her professional career, Robin is the Founder/President of Celebrating Sisterhood and Organizer of SHE SHINES CONFERENCE. She also is the Chief Networking Officer of her boutique consultancy firm, SHINES CONNECTIONS LLC.

Robin earned a Master of Public Administration degree from the University of Delaware and a Bachelor of Science degree in Sociology from Lincoln University. She also earned a Certificate in Biblical Counseling and received an Evangelical Training Association (ETA) Certificate. In 2016, she received her ministerial license.

Robin is a Breast Cancer survivor. She and her family are members of Enon Tabernacle Baptist Church in Philadelphia.

My Pain, His Plan, My Purpose
(Detours to Destiny)
ROBIN SHINE MADDOX

"My mission in life is not merely to survive,
but to THRIVE; and do so with some passion, some compassion,
some humor, and some style." – Maya Angelou

It wasn't until my adult life (in my 50s to be exact) that I realized and embraced my last name: SHINE. Ever since childhood, especially my school age and college years, I would either cringe or feel an "umph" in my stomach whenever my name was mentioned or whenever I had to introduce myself. As I look back on why I "secretly" felt that way, I believe it was a combination of experiences, but mainly what stood out was that I was teased or looked at funny during my school-age years. My classmates would snicker when the teacher called my name during roll call, combined with her pausing while looking up at me before resuming the roll call. Then during recess, while I played jump rope with my friends, the boys would taunt us (as boys do) and yell out my name, "SHINE, HEY SUNSHINE," or "SHINY-HINY," and of course, the laughter would begin. Of course, I laughed it off, but too young then to understand, I internalized being made fun of with embarrassment and shame. It also did not help because of my stature. I was tall for my age, and my hair was very coarse. I regretted getting my hair done with the Vigoral, press and curls, the Dax grease. I was traumatized!! Funny, all those years, what I had perceived as something harmful or "embarrassing" was only an illusion, a lie, a deception. And now I know that God purposely and intentionally had an excellent plan for my life by birthing me into a family whose last name is SHINE!

On June 20, 1963, I was born to Robert and Barbara Shine. The firstborn of four children, my childhood was fulfilling and active. Before my dad's call to pastor a church, we attended a white Baptist church not too far from our home. We were raised in a faith-filled home, and our family was very active in ministry. My siblings and I enjoyed attending and participated in many of the children's ministry activities. We could not wait for Vacation Bible School (VBS) during the summer, where we would invite all of our friends to attend with us. When school resumed in the fall, every Thursday after school, my mom would run us up, along with our friends, and take us to my grandparents' home, where my grandmother, mother, and Rev. Mary Gay would teach us about Jesus using their flannel board and hand puppet props. We would get prizes for scripture memorization and bringing the most friends. Little did I know then that the foundation of my faith was being planted and watered, preparing me for my future – God's purpose and plan for my life (Jeremiah 29:11).

Even though the tenets of my faith were instilled in me when I was young, I had some life experiences that I was not too proud of, which landed me in a state of despair, bewildered, disappointed, struggling, frustrated, and deeply hurt. Those scripture memorizations, thousands of sermons and Sunday School lessons preached and taught, and countless testimonies I heard surfaced as I walked through my adversities, pain, sorrows, and losses. Yet deep within the core of my spirit, I knew, even if my "knowing" was clouded by my circumstances that caused pain, hurt, and were limited to no answers pressured by decisions that had to be made, that somehow, beyond my comprehension, God would bring me through.

I married the love of my life at the age of 27. Both of us were well known within the church community. He played the keyboards, and I was known for directing the choir (many still ask even today, do I direct the choir at my church? Apparently, I must have had a profound effect on folks who have seen me direct choirs.). During our marriage, we were blessed with a daughter after losing four children due to miscarriages. How devasting that was, not one, not two, not three, but FOUR! I recall the first miscarriage. We were just about to leave our home to head to a church in Maryland for a Praise and Worship Conference for music leaders. Our lives were at a crossroads – do we stay home or do we do ministry? I was at a loss, and so was he. We decided to go and so we went. I felt so helpless and bewildered. Powerless because I could not have prevented the loss of our first child. Vulnerable because I did not know how to comfort my husband. Helpless because I did not know how to help myself. Helpless because I could not spare my parents the agony and hurt when we told them the news. After all, they were going to be grandparents for the first time. Not only them, but my siblings, church members, and family and friends were all expecting and anticipating the birth of our child.

Still not understanding and left with the emptiness within, after the third miscarriage, my doctor thought it was best for the both of us to have some tests done to find out what was causing the miscarriages. My husband was incredibly supportive, caring, and loving, to the point that I thought he had dealt with the loss of our children and accepted what God allowed. However, I had no idea he was still dealing with the pain and sorrow of the loss of then three children. It was such a relief when we found out the results of the tests. At least we now had an answer, an explanation. The results found that two of my chromosomes connected, meaning that the tip of two of my chromosomes crossed, attaching itself to the other, thereby causing the miscarriages. Hence, I had a 50/50 chance of carrying to full term. So, as the embryo was developing, it would abort due to the "mismatched" chromosomes. The doctor shared that if the embryo continued to develop and I went to full term delivering the baby, the baby would have so many deformities and health challenges, possibly resulting in death. Now that was a whole lot to take in! We were glad to get an answer to the miscarriages finally, yet we were still emotionally a wreck! So what do we do, do we adopt, do we consider becoming foster parents, use protection from now on, prevent the possibility of me becoming pregnant, do we keep this to ourselves, share with others, and what about our parents?

I would love to share that the news of learning the cause of the many miscarriages was a total relief. No, it just provided the answer to why I was miscarrying the babies we so desired to have. Despite again losing our fourth baby, the pain and sorrow we experienced, and the effects it had on our marital relationship, deep down inside, I came to terms with what God allowed. No, HE did not "ALLOW" this to happen as if HE (God) is mean, cold, callous, and does not care about our feelings, pains, sorrow, and grief. After all, HE is the giver of life! As written in Isaiah 53:3 and Hebrews 4:13, God's only son, Jesus, is acquainted with our pains, sorrows, and grief. I had to understand that God's plans and purposes for my life far exceeded the loss of my four babies, but I would use the losses as means for working everything out for my good and HIS glory (Romans 8:28)! And so HE did, and on October 27, 1995, God blessed us with a 9-pound, 8-ounce baby girl, Raeven Aleia Maddox!! **Remember, GOD'S LIGHT SHINES even when you experience any loss.**

How I wish I could say everything was uphill from there, but I can't. When Raeven was a year and two months, what we thought and were told by her doctor was that she had a bad cold and was given some medicine. One of the members of our church, who called herself Raeven's nanny, came by to check on us, prepare meals, and play with Rae while I took a nap, and noticed that something was wrong. Rae was not herself (she was a happy baby). It was a cold December late afternoon. Her "nanny" insisted that I take Rae to the emergency room. At that time, we lived in Delaware. Not really knowing how to drive a stick shift, I got Rae wrapped in several blankets, jumped in the car, Rae in one hand, (nope, no car seat, I needed her to know that Mommy had her in her arms) while I drove quickly to the hospital. Upon arrival, I checked in. One look at Rae, and they "whisked" her out of my arms, told me to contact my husband, and the rest was…well, let me say, I lived for four months in the hospital. I NEVER left her side.

Raeven contracted strep pneumococcal pneumonia. We were told that babies do not survive with this type of pneumonia. After just a few days at the hospital, we learned that they flew in another baby with the same diagnosis, but she did not make it. I refused to allow the enemy to whisper negative thoughts in my ear and to inflict fear. I got my Bible, wrote every healing scripture I could come across, and taped them to Raeven's bed. While Rae was battling for her life, people worldwide were battling in prayer for her healing. Yes, around the world! I don't know how the news spread to Japan, but we got word that people in Japan heard about Raeven and were praying. One day after the doctors were making their rounds and were speaking to us about Rae's condition, they said she would need a blood transfusion. Upon full explanation, we consented. I decided to walk around the hospital and ran into one of my older cousins, an evangelist. I hadn't seen her in years. We both asked what we were doing at the hospital. She said she worked for a temporary agency, and they assigned her to this hospital in the Phlebotomy department. She said she processed the information for patients scheduled to get blood transfusions and heard about a baby whose life was on the line and needed a transfusion. She shared that she had been praying for this baby, not knowing until she saw tears rolling down my eyes that the baby she was praying for was my daughter, Raeven! Only GOD! She grabbed me by the hand and walked as fast as we could, rushing to get to Rae's room so she could pray! Don't tell me that God does not see, hear, and show himself strongly on our behalf! It was four months long, but I want to say that God is a healer, a sustainer, and is with us during challenging times! OH, did I mention that the church Rease and I were helping out as ministers of music paid every bill that we had! We did not have to concern ourselves with writing out checks every month! They took care of every financial need we had! We did not ask at all. They approached us and told us that is what God laid on their heart to do! **Remember, even in sickness, God's Light SHINES!**

Despite all we experienced, our love and faith in God were intact. Again, I am grateful for the foundation that was laid. I heard time and time again of God's faithfulness, love, mercy, forgiveness, patience, and kindness. Let's not forget about his longsuffering He daily bestows upon us. As Christians, we are to walk by faith and not by sight. When we say we trust him, do we mean it? The testing of our faith is never handed to us on a silver platter. It's never the "warm and fuzzy" moments. It's when we find ourselves in vulnerable, challenging, complex, heart-wrenching, belly aching, teeth clenching, jaw-dropping moments. And the question He whispers in our ears is,

"Do you and will you trust me?" In the most embarrassing, shameful, "how could this happen to me," moments, "Will you trust that I will be here with you to see you through this?" I have experienced that no matter how ugly the situation may be, no matter how much of a struggle and how stressful the situation might become, God does not want us to go through it alone. There's a passage in the Bible, each of us should be reminded of daily, and it is found in Isaiah 43:2-4 (The Message Bible): *"When you're in over your head, I'll be there with you. When you're in rough waters, you will not go down. When you're between a rock and a hard place, it won't be a dead-end—Because I am God, your personal God."* I can attest and bear witness that God is a personal God.

It was in 2012 that twenty-one years of marriage came to a shattering end. No one escaped unscathed and all were scarred in one fashion or another. I was wounded and despondent. If you would ask anyone who knew us, it was a complete shock. There were no "winners." Even while going through the divorce, I made a choice that I would respond (with God's help, overriding my human abilities) through this, still respecting and honoring him as a man and a father. That meant there would be no "baby momma drama" or "being an angry and scornful black woman." I stayed true to my commitment to God and myself and respected my husband, daughter, and extended church family.

Was it challenging at times? Yes! Was I upset and hurt? Yes! Was I resentful in what led to us divorcing? YES! But somehow, I knew that the inner knowing I spoke earlier about was that God was going to take this "mess" and turn it into a message of hope, healing, and restoration. How? At that time, I had no idea, but I can share with you that HE did! It wasn't easy or comfortable, nor did it happen overnight, but HE did it. Much had to do with me being truthful, vulnerable, and most importantly, willing to submit to God's plan, which included a lot of "stripping away," and facing my quirks, attitudes, thoughts, behaviors, and fears.

I will share that many of those within our extended families, friends, acquaintances, and church family did NOT know that I was divorced. Why? Because I chose that we would continue to function as much as a family as we could. That meant holidays, family functions, church, and some events, and we would continue. Now you may be thinking that makes no sense. And, of course, you are correct because that is not how the "world" functions. And as a matter of fact, the Lord spoke to me very clearly: "Robin, this journey that you are now treading has NOTHING to do with making 'sense' but has everything to do with 'making faith!'" I was reminded of a song about faith by Vanessa Bell Armstrong, titled "Faith That Conquers."

Losing our home in the suburbs and moving back home with my parents with a teenager who was about to start high school was humbling. When I informed Rae that we would move in with my parents, I also said, "I don't know how or when, but we will have our place." I repeated that to her time and time again. I kept telling her that the Lord would bless us with a place of our own to live. And when that time came, we, along with everyone else, would know it was God. As we lived off my income, paid back accumulated debt, paid for ongoing car repairs, and just basic living expenses, I continued to trust God. I will never forget one evening when my phone rang, and I decided not to answer because I knew the purpose of the call and that it was on my schedule to call the person the following day to inform her that we were all set for a scheduled meeting. Well, the person was persistent and kept calling until I finally answered. While she told me why she was calling, I told her that we were set for the meeting. We both were talking at the same time. I finally stopped talking, and she said, "That is NOT the reason I called." She said she was persistent because she was sitting at her table praying to ask God who she could offer a consulting contract to for a short-term project, and my name kept coming to mind, so that was her reason for calling me. I propped myself up and wanted to be clear about what she was saying. She responded by saying God told her to offer me a contract for a large amount of money to take this project. It was a simple, straightforward project, and she said that if I accepted, she would send me the contract, make it effective immediately and send me a retainer check! I was speechless, to say the least, while tears were running down my face. She had NO idea of my situation, but God knew! I could not wait until the next day to share with Rae that God saw our need, answered my prayers and that we could begin looking for a home once I paid off my debt!

I thank God for the type of parents I have. Even while I was going through the divorce, they never spoke ill of my husband or me. He is still engaged and viewed as part of the family. There were many losses and heartaches as I was going through a divorce, but I can say we are friends, and I never interfered but supported and made sure that he continued engaging in Raeven's life, even to this day, now that she is a young adult. We made it known that even though Mommy and Daddy were no longer married, we both still loved her and would parent her until death does us apart. Nope, there was no playing one parent against the other (she tried but found out quickly that was not going to work!).

Those things that I lost due to going through a divorce, over time, God restored. I believe that because I trusted HIM and demonstrated my trust by responding accordingly, HE honored and favored me. We live in our home; my ex-husband and I are still friends, and we continue to schedule time with the three of us. Even going through separation and divorce, God is still with us. Remember, God supplies every one of our needs according to HIS riches in glory! While we are trying to figure it out, God has already worked it out. He uses people, and not always the people we know personally. Is there pain in the suffering? YES. Is there heartache, hurt, disappointment, fear, confusion, questioning, bewilderment? YES! Your journey will include all of this and more…detours, delays, denials, but know that your pain is creating a platform for you to pursue the purpose God has for you if you trust HIS process and carry out the plan HE has for your life!

"As you look back and reflect upon your past, thank God. As you look forward, trust God. As you look around, serve God. Always look within and find God."

As women, at least once a year, we see our doctor(s) and are encouraged to get our check-ups and screenings. I had a routine for scheduling my yearly appointments, exams, and screenings. Each time I went, I received the same results, except for my gaining a few pounds here and there. But that was NOT the case on February 26, 2018. This time, I was told that I had breast cancer. I will never forget that day. My mother was with me when my doctor informed me of my diagnosis. When she confirmed the test results, we were silent for a second, then I immediately, without hesitation, asked if I could pray for her hands. She consented; I began to pray. While praying, God had me pray not only for her hands but for her mind and the knowledge she obtained back when she was in medical school. I asked the Lord to bring back everything she studied, information obtained from medical conferences, seminars, research studies, conversations with her medical colleagues. I thanked the Lord for her and all her preparation which led her to this time. After the prayer, my mother asked her if she was a believer in Jesus Christ, and she said she was. I then said, let's schedule the surgery. And so we did.

Talk about timing—well, can I share that my pre-operation was scheduled the day following Rae's spring break from college. You see, she was in her last year of college, and on that snowy Thursday night, I picked Rae up from college. I planned to break the news to her as we traveled home, but that did not happen. As soon as Rae got into the car, she shared excitement that she was accepted into a sorority. She was overjoyed! There was NO way I could mention my diagnosis and date of surgery to a college student who just got accepted into a sorority! "Lord, this timing is not going well," I whispered.

What should I do? I had to be at the hospital at 7:30 am! I was at my wit's end. Well, after another hour or so talking about her acceptance and all that she needed to do to get prepared, I finally shared with her that I had something very important to share. Let's say, once I shared the news, she went from being happy and excited to immediately into shock. Tears were rolling from her eyes so fast that her face was wet; her body started shaking. All I could do was to hold her tightly and hum while praying for God to HELP! I did not know what to say or do. Then, in a still, small voice, the Lord told me to call a therapist who was on standby. I had forgotten that I had called her and asked for her assistance if I needed to tell Rae. My therapist friend immediately picked up the phone and spoke with Rae while I held onto her tightly. Once the call ended, I told her, "God is going to heal me." I kept telling her that, like before, God was with us and would see us through.

I came through surgery fine. My parents, Raeven, and Rease were with me. When they rolled me into surgery, one of the staff personnel was a young lady I knew from church. Once again, God made his presence known. I had my cellphone talking to two friends, laughing and reassuring them that God was with me and I would be ok. The nurse took the phone from my hands, applied oxygen over my nose, and off to sleep I went.

It was a long, painful life staring at the death moment, but God told me, "You are not going to die but live to declare the works of God! This pain creates a platform that will bring you before many people to inspire, empower, and offer hope! You will be a light SHINING in many spaces and places where there is hopelessness, darkness, and despair; where people need to know that they matter." That all sounded great, and I looked forward to what was said; however, I had to experience some things on my road to recovery. Chemotherapy and radiation caused my breathing to be labored. It was challenging to move around, to walk. I was out of breath even trying to get out of bed. I spent most of my time in bed. I was fragile; I could not even eat – everything I attempted to eat or drink (water, even Ensure) all tasted like metal. Yet, God once again was with me and showed himself as a healer and provider. Can I testify? I wanted for nothing! Every need was supplied! I experienced so much support and love from so many people. My daughter was able to pledge the sorority; she never missed any of her classes and graduated on time. Still recovering, I made sure she was celebrated; I was asked to post a video about the importance of health insurance and did not realize over a thousand people watched the video on a social media platform; I was interviewed by one of the oldest newspapers in Philadelphia; I was the recipient of the PINK Ribbon Award presented by the Pennsylvania Breast Cancer Coalition and now was just asked to serve on their board; and one of the greatest highlights is that during my recovery in 2019, I hosted my inaugural conference, SHE SHINES!

So you see, no matter what the adversity, challenge, or loss, God keeps his promises. He is there with us through it all. He takes a mess and turns it into a message of HOPE and INSPIRATION so that we can let our light SHINE!!!

Keep moving forward while you are in pain, until your pain becomes your past. In pain, you will discover how strong you are and how

God will grant you the strength you need for every step of your journey. Your past creates a platform for you to propel forward with courage and the ability to inspire, help, and offer hope to others, while experiencing the blessings and favor of God. SHINE YOUR LIGHT BRIGHTLY, and just in case your light gets dim, flickers, or goes out, quickly strike a match and light a candle and SHINE!!

Jerri St. John was born in New Jersey, raised in California, and has made her home in Maryland for the past thirty years. She is an empty-nester, married to her best friend, a mother and grandmother. Jerri has been on her own since the age of sixteen. Having experienced many hardships throughout her life, she has overcome the challenges of depression, morbid obesity, childhood abuse, and domestic violence. Her life's passion and purpose are inspiring and coaching other women with hope, confidence and love.

As the owner of JewelsfromJerri, LLC, Jerri is a Certified Life Coach, Podcast Host, Social Media Influencer, and Independent Stylist with Color Street, who strives to be a light in the world; spreading joy, hope and positivity. She considers her strong faith, optimism, love of people and her positive outlook to be her greatest strengths.

Contact Jerri at: jewelsfromjerri@gmail.com or through her website at http://innersparkle.net

From Broken to Bad-A$$

JERRI ST. JOHN

Growing up in a war zone, I was on high alert all of the time. Every little noise, movement, doors opening, were all signals that something could be going on that required me to hide or to protect myself. My household of origin was one that created this sense of fear. I spent most of my time hiding in my room—alone—playing with my paper dolls, reading books, singing, or outside with the neighborhood kids playing hide and seek. NO, it wasn't a REAL war zone, but one created by the adults in my home where there was never a safe space, a safe moment or any stability. I anticipated something going wrong at every turn and usually I was still unprepared for what was to follow. People who experience war suffer from PTSD. My life was filled with trauma and I lived on the precipice of despair and fear for as long as I can remember. I had an absentee father who worked two jobs to put food on the table, while my mother spent most of her days hiding in the bedroom or away from the house. I spent most of my time with my wonderful Nana, the only safe haven in my life – the grand-mother who raised the woman who gave birth to me. She was the first and (for quite some time) ONLY person in my life who loved me unconditionally, enjoyed my company, spent time getting to know me and never judged me. Nana allowed me to experience real love and became the surrogate mother that I so desperately craved.

I always felt lonely. I always felt like an outsider. I never fit in. Even though I was outgoing and friendly, I had very few friends. My mother was Jewish, my father was Protestant and I grew up confused, with no basis of values or beliefs in my life. We celebrated Hanukkah but it was more about the gifts than anything else. On Christmas we would visit my father's sister and celebrate. I always enjoyed the Christmas carols, the decorations and the trees and wondered why we were the only house on the block that did not have a Christmas tree and colorful lights. At the age of seven, I found out that being Jewish was something I needed to hide. My father had bought me a Star of David and I wore it to school one day. On my way home, as I was crossing the playground, three kids accosted me, pushed me down, spit on me, called me a "dirty Jew," and yanked that necklace from my neck. That day, I disavowed anything to do with Judaism and refused to acknowledge that I was Jewish by birth. We never learned anything about our religion or customs so it only meant pain to me. It was something that apparently was shameful. Following this incident, I retreated into myself even more and became more lonely than ever.

My mother spent many days hiding in her room. Her excuses were headaches or the need to "sleep in." I realized years later that she was relying on prescription medications to cope with her life and spent most of her days in bed. While my mother was avoiding her life, I was taking on the responsibilities of caring for my two younger brothers. One was still in diapers and needed changing. The other needed breakfast and help getting out the door to school. I learned to take on responsibilities far beyond my years and was grateful for the escape when I left for school each weekday. This home environment prevented me from having sleepovers or friends come over to play and required a lot of creativity on my part to get together with friends. My father was rarely home. I was virtually becoming an adult way before I was capable of making adult decisions, with two "parents" who were not only emotionally unavailable, but also physically unavailable as well. I was a "good" girl. I loved school, got good grades, cherished my few close friends, and spent most of my time caring for my two younger brothers. Time spent outside the home and school was spent getting away from the stress, neglect and strain of our environment. I went to the local creek and caught tadpoles. I climbed trees, played kickball and found ways to escape whenever possible. There was always the threat of "wait until your father gets home" looming over my head if something did not go quite right during the day. My father was the disciplinarian and the favored method of punishment was pulling my pants down, pushing me face-down on a bed and brutally beating me with his belt. The tension of listening to him remove the belt from his belt loops created anxiety and unimaginable fear. No matter what I did, it was never enough. When I received good grades, they were never good enough. I was never thin enough, pretty enough, smart enough, well-behaved enough or helpful enough. I spent my entire life expecting perfection from myself and always seeking my parents' approval…yet it was NEVER enough.

My truly happy memories come from the times I would walk down the street to my Nana and Papa's house. Our immediate family rarely spent time together. When we did, my grandparents were usually present and my joy came from annual treks to Disneyland, swimming in my grandparents' pool or sharing meals with them. With my father working two or three jobs to pay the bills, we never had a family vacation or any luxuries. A special treat was an ice cream from the Good Humor Man. Nana and Papa provided those extras.

I sought out the attention of boys at a very young age. I was a "tomboy" but was also called "boy crazy" in my pre-teens and found out early that I was able to feel better about myself by using my body to get attention. With no parents around to supervise my activities, I found myself experimenting in dark rooms, touching, kissing and receiving the attention that I so desperately craved. This behavior led to immediate gratification but also created feelings of shame, guilt and self-loathing that I did not comprehend at the time. I went on a long journey of self-destructive behavior that lasted well into adulthood. If I was expected to be an adult, then I would enjoy some of the experiences that adults enjoyed. With little to no supervision, I was left to my own devices. I believe that this time in my life was when the depression began, but because I grew up at a time when mental illness was not discussed or acknowledged, it was all chalked up to being a "moody teenager."

Abuse, neglect, lack of love, molestation by male babysitters, a near-rape while home alone with my little brothers one night, parents sweeping EVERYTHING under the rug because somehow, this MUST have been my fault; I must have asked for it...I kept getting the messages that I just was not important. I was irrelevant. I was not ENOUGH. I was being told in SO many ways that I was there just to serve my parents' whims. Then my world came crashing down! You might be thinking that this world was already pretty shaky, but my parents informed me that they were separating. I was grateful for this news because it meant that the house might be quiet. Maybe I would not be receiving any more beatings. Maybe some of the yelling, fighting and chaos would cease.

My mother got a job. My father moved out of our home. He began making attempts to be my buddy and both of them worked on convincing me that they were the better parent. After years of my father being emotionally unavailable and abusive, he wanted me to forget everything and start going to basketball games, visiting him at work and hanging out together. I was afraid of my father and I did not trust him. My mother became even more unavailable as she started dating almost immediately and was never at home. She moved a married man into our apartment and started living as though she were a teenager again. All of this while I was in high school, ready to start attending school dances, having friends and dating myself. All of that was put on hold because I had to stay home, yet again, to take care of my brothers. Then my Papa died. It was the most heartbreaking event of my young life and created such additional chaos in our family that my already fragile existence became threatened in many more dramatic ways.

So many years of stunted emotional growth, needing approval and acceptance, and experiencing self-loathing led to more years of self-destructive behavior. The cliché of "Sex, Drugs and Rock & Roll" would define my latter teen and early adult years. I started working and was living on my own at seventeen years old. Experimenting with drugs and relationships that were abusive were habits that lasted well into my thirties. I am so grateful that God was watching out for me because some of the impulsive decisions that I made could have caused me harm or even death. I continually attracted people into my life who were replicas of my parents and married four times before I finally realized that my behavior needed to change. I was forced to give up custody of my son in the turmoil of one of the divorces.

Broken and bruised from a life of pain, I met the love of my life in 1991. Impulsively, I moved from California to Maryland after only two months. I am so grateful that the ONE time that I trusted my intuition and listened to what could have only been God nudging me in this direction, I found growth, healing and my future. We were married a year later and went through some rough years that strengthened our relationship and helped us grow as a couple and as individuals. He loved and accepted me the way that my amazing Nana did years ago. This relationship finally provided me with the ability to be myself and begin the healing process. We built a life together, adopted a beautiful daughter, bought our own home, and struggled with finances and family drama. Together we navigated a diagnosis of my depression. Our marriage almost did not survive. I spent nearly twenty years on anti-depressants and in treatment to never quite get it right until I made the decision that I did not want to live this way any longer. Thanks to our faith, God and my husband, we are stronger than ever.

I entered a new world of feelings when I made the decision to stop the anti-depressants and face life "au naturel." I expected to suddenly be cured – free from the anger, pain and sadness that had consumed my life for so long. In reality, even though I had been on anti-depressants for twenty years, with a diagnosis of clinical depression, I am convinced that I went undiagnosed for at least an equal amount of time prior to that diagnosis. It explains so much about my younger years, my relationships and my choices. When I operated from a place of fear, anxiety and depression, my choices were often self-destructive.

I had been told all of my life that I wasn't ENOUGH!

As I emerged from the protective cocoon of the anti-depressants, I realized that this was an uphill battle. I had not allowed myself to feel for years. I had not cried. Suddenly I was terrified! My heart was racing; I felt a tightness in my chest, a churning in my gut. I had trouble catching my breath. What if I could not function without the anti-depressants? What if I got lost back in the darkness of that depression, never to emerge again? The only feelings I had for years were feelings of anger and rage. The rage was directed at everyone close to me, pushing them away, keeping them at arm's length because then I could prove my parents right – I WASN'T good enough. I was not worthy of love. The rage I was feeling was an inner anger at having no control over my thoughts, feelings or actions due to the demon depression. My behavior became self-destructive self-abuse that permeated my soul and kept me trapped inside all of that pain.

The healing began the day I made the decision to stop putting chemicals into my body and begin the hard work of finding out what makes me tick. I began to slowly understand who was in this body and mind. What I was not prepared for was the lengthy process of rediscovery, rebirth and growth. I expected to be well as soon as the medication was out of my system. Instead, I became fearful, confused and terrified of life without my crutch!

"You've been numbed out by those antidepressants for years. You haven't been feeling. Be kind to yourself. This will take some time. These things you're feeling are normal and you will be OK," my beautiful, compassionate acupuncturist reassured me.

WOW!!!

Feelings…

Numbness…

Fear…

These were all new to me. I was not sure how to process this. I no longer had the security of hiding behind my medication. It had been the only thing that kept me out of hiding, preventing me from crawling into bed and pulling the covers up over my head, and keeping me from checking out of life for days on end.

My greatest fear was that I would plunge back into that darkness, never to return again. That this time would be irreversible. That there would be no turning back and no one would be able to save me.

I put one foot in front of the other, holding my breath, afraid every time I got a little bit sad, convinced that the depression was ready to take over. I continued my acupuncture treatment weekly for several months and eventually realized that it was acceptable to have a bad day or even a rough week. It was not the harbinger of the depression returning to ravage my psyche and soul once again.

As the years passed and I am still free from medication and depression, I have learned that my mindset is critical. Mindset and a strong faith account for 90% of my optimistic, joyous outlook on life. Waking up grateful to be alive, starting the day with energy and positivity empowers me to participate in life purposefully and productively. I have learned to practice self-care and self-awareness. These are definitely learned behaviors. While I considered myself intelligent and "street smart," I needed to learn to accept and love myself BECAUSE of my imperfections, not in spite of them.

Is life perfect? OF COURSE NOT! It IS pretty awesome!

Thanks to my faith, God and my husband, my marriage and all of my relationships are stronger than ever. I am so blessed and grateful to have had my wonderful husband with me every step of the way.

I am now able to discern when I need time to unwind or rejuvenate. I am able to embrace the rough times and accept that it is all part of the ups and downs of life. Most of my days are filled with optimism and happiness. I now have the ability to find the positive in every situation and to move forward before I get stuck in the mire.

I am "Free to Fly." Some days I choose to walk, ride or even rest. It is now all about the daily choices I make for the greater good. I have learned to practice daily, healthy habits that keep me moving forward. I pray, practice positive affirmations, journal regularly, and have worked on re-parenting myself to undo the damage that was done by people who did the best they could. I have practiced forgiveness and gratitude. I have forgiven those who have "wronged" me but more importantly, I have forgiven myself for being a fragile human being who had to go through these trials and struggles in order to come out the other side.

Learning to ask for what I need, giving myself permission to feel and setting boundaries in my relationships has been crucial to my ability to thrive rather than simply survive.

It is still a process of daily self-discovery. An important lesson that I have learned is that no one else can tell me who I should be, how I should act or what I should think. My past no longer defines me. Everything that God has led me through has been to provide strength and empower me. I have grown into a self-aware, happy, joyous woman who believes in her own strength and inner beauty.

Now that I have accepted and love the woman I have become, I am better able to fulfill my purpose here on this earth. I am no longer afraid of being enough! I have learned to trust that God will bring me through my trials with greater awareness, strength, and courage to face whatever life brings. I bring the best version of ME to life and to others every single day.

What's so awesome about this is that once I recognized my true value in this world, I was able to discover my purpose. My true purpose and passion is to inspire other women. Nothing is impossible with

God's help. I want to pass this message of hope, confidence and love on to others who are struggling to let them know that there are blessings on the other side of the fear, anxiety, depression and trauma.

Today I have hope! Today I have faith! Today I love and believe in myself! Today I accept myself for who and what I am. Today I have value! Today I am loved! It took work, faith and strength that I received from going through the experiences that I did throughout my life! I have no regrets about my past. I view everything as experiences that were needed to get me to where I am today. Everything that we overcome in this life is a lesson. Some lessons are needed to build our character and strengthen us. Do I wish that some things had not happened? Not necessarily. I would not be who I am today if not for the tapestry of all of my life's journeys.

It took me until I was in my sixties to finally grasp that I am not only worthy, but that I have fabulous gifts and talents to offer the world. I no longer allow the inner voices and limiting beliefs of my past to intrude on what needs to be done. Today, I am unapologetically and proudly 100% ME and I encourage YOU to find that inner strength and beauty that is within each and every one of you to become the amazing person you were meant to be.

Perita H. Adams is a Certified Christian Life & Business Coach. She holds an Associate Degree in International Business and a Bachelor Degree in Organizational Communication. After studying abroad and missionary work in Africa, Brazil, Canada, China, Ecuador and many other countries, she recognized her calling to inspire, educate, and motivate women to tap into their God-given gifts and talents to fulfill God's plan and purpose in their lives.

Perita is the owner of "GeneSIS Beginning Coaching & Consulting LLC." She has held many women's conferences and is a three-time bestselling author. In recent she has created a powerful 4-week course entitled "Birds of a Feather" created on the essence of "taking flight" in your life and letting strongholds go. This program was so well received that she is currently working on Part 2.

Perita is a native of North Carolina. In her down-time she enjoys, reading, writing, art and spending time with her family. If you are interested in coaching, or booking her for speaking engagements you may do so at:

The GeneSIS Beginning Coaching & Consulting LLC.
10130 Perimeter Parkway, Suite 200
Charlotte, NC 28216
Website: thegenesisbeginning.com
Email: thegenesisbeginning@yahoo.com
FB: Perita "Juju" Adams
LinkedIn: https://www.linkedin.com/in/perita-adams-446193203/
IG: https://www.instagram.com/peritaadams/

The Making of a Queen Who Beat the Odds!

PERITA ADAMS

As I start my story. I decide to look up the world's meaning of the term "**queen**" which reads, "the female ruler of an independent state, especially one who inherits the position by **right of birth**." That definition sounds pretty good. However, I continue to dig deeper and find another meaning which reads, "the most **POWERFUL** chess piece that each player has, able to move any number of unobstructed squares in any direction along a rank, file, or diagonal on which it stands." Bingo! That's my story. (Oxford Languages)

Reflecting on the world's perception of **queendom** helps me to ascertain how women of power are viewed. However, I know full well who we are and were created to be: powerful, wise, beautiful and confident women, the epitome of God's very best. So with the knowledge of what we as women represent and are capable of, why do we tend to succumb and think less of our ability to exude **GREATNESS**?

As a young girl I would often question my gifts and talents. Sure, I was good at writing, painting, and creativity but what was my true genius? To be completely honest, I was quite shy. That may seem hard to believe. However, what I've come to see now is that shyness was a mask for lack of confidence. So I blew people off the map another way using written words. In grade school I received several awards for creative writing and expressive art. You see, I mention this because as a woman your voice can be heard many different ways. If you are a seamstress or fashion designer your designs are your voice to the world, or if you are a great cook your voice can be heard in the delicious food you present and provide, etc.

Just as the name of my company, "The GeneSIS Beginning," exudes to all things in life, there is a beginning and here is my road to **Queendom**. Many times, I have spoken of my grandmother, the mother of 13 children. She was organized, wise, and observant. To look at her you wouldn't know she had any children. I often wondered how she was able to pull off such a balancing act. My grandmother was a registered nurse, mom, wife and entrepreneur. With all the hats she wore it was almost impossible to keep up with her, but the hat that stood out to me the most was her crown. So I decided to watch her, this matriarch, and our "**QUEEN**." The funny part is little did I know that she was training me to be a **QUEEN** as well.

As a child I was often sick with various health concerns, one of which was Endometriosis, a female issue that tried to physically kill me. But my grandmother would tell me how strong, resilient and wise I was, so I had very little time to pity myself. She was great at coaching me to be my best self. There's no wonder why I'm a diligent coach. So I planned to follow my grandmother around for at least a week, starting the following week. Bright and early that following Monday morning my journey (queendom training) began. Just as the rooster crowed at 5:00 am sharp I heard my grandmother's feet hit the floor, so I jumped up to get into position. Mind you, I slept in my clothes because I knew she was an early riser. Funny, I know, but reality. I dragged myself into the kitchen and there she was on her way to the henhouse and back to the kitchen to cook breakfast before I could even get my boots on. She would always stay informed with the current news, so it was always Maxwell House Coffee and the paper . for her every morning during breakfast. Next out to the garden and cornfield at 6:00 am, planting, pruning, and gathering, then back inside to clean everything she harvested from the garden. She carried on like that all day long doing household chores, washing clothes, fixing lunch, etc., but I kept up. Midday she did banking and shopping for the best deals for the family. She always shopped in bulk; now so do I. Problem is, I only have one child but it helps me to be a blessing to others. She had three different bank accounts, although I was too young to understand. I knew she was making power moves because I listened in as she spoke to the banker. Her daily grind was tough but she never wavered. I was pooped trying to keep up with her!

However, what surprised me most about my grandmother was her eloquence and power by just utilizing a few short words. She could speak to people on many different levels, a quality she trained in me. Her presence was strong and regal. She was a beautiful light-skinned, medium-built woman with dark wavy hair. She was cute but commanded order and often times got it, not as a bully but as a "**QUEEN**" who knew how to adjust her position on the board no matter what she was doing. Often she would have dinner parties and have us dress up in formal dresses and serve party trays with finger sandwiches and such, always instilling etiquette in her grandchildren. She was raising "**Queens**" and we knew it. Her crown was big and beautiful, adorned with many rubies representing every level she had achieved.

Now that you know my foundation, here's my story. Referring back to the definition of a "**queen**" as one who receives that by right of birth, my grandmother relinquished her crown to me about two years ago as she passed away. Much like the second definition, I felt like I moved around my chess board forward, backward, and diagonally like my grandmother as a "**queen**" trying to keep my position as "**Queen Who Defied the Odds.**"

Confidence is key when you are fighting for your position. In life many things will try to steal your crown from you and catch you off guard. I know this because like many of you, I endured some comparable battles, taking note of the fact that my physical ailments almost killed me, my mother was physically and mentally abused, I was deemed unfertile, and I had open-heart surgery—all by the age of 30. When you look at those kinds of odds life looks pretty brutal. But I never gave up my voice, my courage and most of all my crown.

You see, I learned to look at life a different way. Sure, I was extremely sick but I was among the living. God had placed greatness in me and my grandmother watered, nurtured, and cultivated it just like the gardens and fields she tended to daily. My grandmother and "**queen**" made sure I kept my hand on the plow and pushed forward at all times. There was no time to look back; that would've been unproductive in her eyes. However, understand sometimes the plow may be heavy because the dirt in your life that you have to move is hard and sometimes you want to give up but keep pushing; you're breaking new ground.

Jesus replied, "No one who puts a hand to the plow and looks back is fit for service in the kingdom of God." Luke 9:62, NIV So my advice to you is not to look back; your blessing is ahead of you.

Can I be real with you? Let me tell you I often wanted to put that plow down because life can be heavy sometimes, but I knew in order to reap the harvest the ground has to be prepared so I kept pushing, praying and looking out for God's promises.

There will be times that you want to look back and go back to the life you knew. Some might call it a "Comfort Level" but if it was comfortable, you would've never left.

My mom was, is, and forever will be a praying mother. Although her strength wasn't as pronounced as my grandmother, her crown is adorned with crosses. She always told us that we were "The King's Kids." Her "**queendom**" is filled with biblical scripture, prayer, and steadfastness. Many times, as a young girl I viewed my mother as weak and afraid. But as I observed her, I realized that she was grounded, determined and strong. She always thought of her children first and provided for us even if it meant staying in a toxic relationship and sacrificing herself. So for those of you going through similar circumstances, hang in there; you're stronger than you think!

Nevertheless, my mother didn't have to stay. Her family was more than equipped to help her leave but she felt stuck and lost her sense of worth. She, like most women, hoped things would turn around and she'd be able to proudly wear her crown but it would never happen in this abusive situation. However, what would happen was as she ministered to her daughters, she inadvertently would discover her own value as a "**QUEEN**" and take her position in the game of life as the most powerful piece on the board.

"An excellent woman (one who is spiritual, capable, intelligent, and virtuous), who is he who can find her? Her value is more precious than jewels *and* her worth is far above rubies or pearls." Proverbs 31:10, AMP

So my mother placed a cross of wisdom on my crown as she helped me to understand who I was and who I belonged to. I am the daughter of the "King of all Kings." She fulfilled her charge as a "**queen**" by teaching us the things to accept and not accept, leading by example.

With my mother's training I stand strong as an activist for women's rights and the betterment of women, always instilling in women the power of their voice and their genius. I have even often traveled to Africa and various countries such as Brazil, Ecuador and many others to help women understand their value and seek out their divine gifts and talents. I also teach them the importance of loving themselves as well as taking pride in their appearance so that they can be a beacon of hope to their daughters. Not to mention many platforms here in the States such as the YWCA (Young Women's Christian Association), known as a global organization that aims to advance the empowerment, rights, and leadership of women, young women and girls in over 120 countries. I held a "Women's Empowerment" event along with another collaborator in the Charlotte, N.C. area a few years back.

I did all of this while still fighting to hold onto my crown. In early 2000 another blow came upon me and I transitioned my course on the board by moving diagonally to avoid the inevitable. My heart was in trouble. I needed surgery and without it, I would experience sudden death. This was a battle I wasn't prepared for but nonetheless I knew in order to win I needed to stay confident, strategic, and prayed up. At the time my son was only six years old and again I tapped into my grandmother's training: no time for pity, adjust your crown and take your position. You may wonder how I remained calm and steadfast with news of this nature. My answer is by remaining educated about my body. For every answer they gave me I had another question, until I was well-informed of the potential outcomes. I stayed inspired by praying, reading the word, and having personal conversations with God. I stayed motivated by using affirmations such as *I can beat this, Greater is He who is in me than He who is in the world, my body is healthy and so is my heart,* etc.

Today I stand victorious as a "**queen**" who won that battle. You see, I was born with an anomaly, which means no one knew how my heart was built except God. My heart was functioning fine; it was just that the right and left arteries of the heart were on the same side. The doctors couldn't believe what they were seeing. I had made it to the age of 30 without this being detected. How? God has a time for everything in life, and it wasn't my time.

With COVID-19 slowly moving behind us, one thing I know for sure is how valuable time is. I often tell my clients, "Don't let your genius go unseen; invest in yourself. Learn how to tap into your gifts and talents because someone somewhere is waiting to benefit from your greatness." Sometimes because we have lost our voice or position as a "**queen,**" we need the accountability of a coach or mentor who can teach us how to wear our crown as well as how to keep it against all odds.

Divorce is the bad "D" word. Nobody wants to make a mistake and most of all nobody, especially a Christian woman, wants to have that on her record. I was no exception to the rule. I was married for 10 years to my child's father, and letting go was one of the hardest things I had to do in my life. For me there was no one to blame; it was just the end. An ending like this in life can make you question your worth, your value, your spiritual position with God, because you see, I took it to heart that I had made a "vow," a promise to God to do everything perfect. But what I later realized was that I didn't live in a perfect world. To this very day I still don't condone families being torn apart. I love the comment that Kirk Franklin gave a few months back regarding his disagreement with his son. He said, "I'm just an imperfect man trying to serve a perfect God."

You see, a woman's crown can be uncomfortable at times. Some of them are heavy from burdens: divorce, abuse, low self-esteem, financial hardship etc. Nevertheless, we must learn to wear them with confidence. Crowns are a symbol of our strength, power, and beauty.

I love trivia and, as you have guessed, being educated. Did you know that the gems on a queen's crown represent achievement? The crown also represents the dignity of the queen. In fact, Queen Elizabeth's crown from the people of Burma was adorned with over 96 rubies and her Imperial State Crown has 2868 Diamonds, 17 Sapphires, 11 Emeralds, and 269 Pearls, as well as other gemstones. This is how valuable we are as women (queens)—worthy to take our position on any given day.

Today, I'm a woman on a mission to inspire, educate, and motivate women while teaching them the power of confidence. I have a son whom we adopted as a baby who has a beautiful spirit. Many times, I like to say he was specially chosen for us and we were chosen for him. I didn't allow the divorce to take my position as a wonderful mother and co-parent. Even when the world said "unfertile," God said "special delivery." When the doctors scratched their heads over my heart issue being undiscovered for over 30 years, God said, "I am the creator and great physician. Her heart is just fine. I made her that way." No one can understand God's great mysteries. My mother and I are best friends. She has lived many years free from her abuser who has since passed away.

Humility and humbleness are key. All my gems and the structure of my crown didn't come without life's trials. But I'm grateful for the lessons and the resilience my grandmother cultivated in me. Now with God's blessing I'm a three-time best-selling author. I hold a B.A. in Communications, an Associate's in International Business, and many other certifications. I've been honored on the dean's list and president's list several times. I've crossed cultural barriers for the betterment of women, and I'm just beginning. I thoroughly enjoy answering the call to establish The GeneSIS Beginning Coaching & Consulting, LLC, helping women live purposeful, confident, and rewarding lifestyles in life and business.

My crown is full of great achievements and some of my gems were extremely hard to get. But what I know for sure is just like me, you too deserve to wear your crown with dignity and grace. Many times, the world may try to say "she's not good enough, she's not strong enough, she's too sick, she's not smart enough, she's broken, she's not pretty enough," etc. and when this happens, I want you to simply say, "**I'm a queen**; who I can be is up to me." You can do it!

You want to know how I know? Because I'm a **"QUEEN and I Defied the Odds."**

Welcome home **"Queens;"** your queendom awaits.

Special Recognition to the following women's organizations who are mentoring and inspiring **"Queens"** and countless other organizations who stand for the advancement of womanhood.

ABWA- American Business Women's Association
YWCA- Young Women's Christian Association
FAITH AT WORK Television Show-Yvette Gavin
The Battered Women's Shelter
The Endometriosis Foundation of America
Jesus, Coffee & Prayer-Minister Nakita Davis
In Her Shoes Movement
(NAWBO) National Association of Women Business Owners
Women in the World Foundation

Apostle Donna-Jeanne Christopher, Th.D.

Dr. Donna-Jeanne Christopher was ordained a Reverend (2007); Graduated with Doctorate of Theology (2011). Passionate about following the LORD, Donna-Jeanne is Empowering, Loving, Liberating, Leading & Launching God's Leaders through the Word so they Operate in Total Healing while Making Disciples of Others through the Doctrine of Christ Jesus. She is consistently moving them into their God-Given Destiny w/Purpose.

Dr. Donna-Jeanne Christopher is CEO & Cofounder of KOGIAH Inc., (International Healing Ministries). God has moved through her to birth Ministries, Churches, and a School. Currently she sits with & councils various ministries in the United States and abroad. She travels extensively throughout the United States and in foreign lands instructing, exhorting and strategizing through the Word of God. She is married to Rev. Eric T. Christopher, Pastor.

Life Scriptures: Galatians 2:20; John 10:37; 1John 2:20

Visit her website for more information.

www.donnajeanneministries.org
donnajeannneministries@gmail.com
267-402-8732

Life

APOSTLE DR. DONNA-JEANNE CHRISTOPHER

Life happens. No denying it. No ignoring it. It doesn't go away. It doesn't disappear. No matter how far you go, it will always show up. I am not talking about your everyday breathing in and breathing out life. I am referring to the 'life' that forms who you are (your experiences) and how these experiences challenge your very belief system—the same belief system, by the way, that you have invented and put in place as a survival mechanism. The system you fall back on when you begin to think that the rainbow just may not have been enough. And you begin to think "Hmmmm, so now what do I do?"

I found myself in just that place when my husband and I became the fulltime caregivers for my parents. Unexpectedly. Out of the blue. Not really seeing it coming (knowing that your parents are 'getting up there'). Watching them out of the side of your eye yet standing firm on the fact that it's Mom and Dad. No matter what, they have always been ok. So they always will. Right???

Care Giving w/Love – A few lessons on Life. On January 9, 2010, I remember immediately after waking (while still lying in my bed), reminiscing about a few things. Here are just a couple of those thoughts…

WOW...is it really morning already? Seems like I just closed my eyes. Lots to do today. People will be here soon. I suspect lots and lots of people. This house will most likely have more people in it today than I have seen since I returned here almost seven years ago. Come on, girl, get it together. Today, of all days, is not the time to find yourself all over the place. Not today, girl, not today! You have to speak in about four hours and you have absolutely no idea what you are going to say.

There I go again. So many memories here—makes it hard to stay focused on the matters at hand. And just about all of them involve family one way or another. Amazing, delicious dinners and beautiful graduations and exciting birthdays and unbelievable Christmases and unforgettable weddings and joyous births and painful funerals and sad goodbyes. All part of life. Somehow, I managed to navigate them all while keeping my eye on the rainbow, up to now. So how did I wind up here, in this place of sadness? Feeling rejected, abandoned and worthless? As if I have nothing of any value to offer anyone. It's taken me a while to figure out that I need courage to confront my past. Courage to forgive. Courage to acknowledge my part in it all and courage to acknowledge everyone else's.

I always wanted to know what it was about me that caused my mom to call me. I was the farthest away. I was like the black sheep because of my past. Suddenly I get the call and my husband and I wind up here. Now seven years have passed. The times of caregiving. What a journey this has been. Mom told me that "I was the one." I never understood what she meant, until now. Funny how Mom used to tell me often that I should go to nursing school (she knew even then – that mother's discernment). And I would always laugh. "Not me, Mommy," I'd shout! "I ain't cleaning up nobody's poop or looking at any blood or washing someone's private parts or cleaning up some- one's drool or giving no enema's or, I don't really know what else; I just know it's not me." And that's what I would tell her, each and every time. And she would undoubtedly say, "But you're the one!"

One thing for sure, this bed sure feels better than the floor. Lying here and listening to the noise over my head, I am just sooo glad to be in a bed. Even so, I am gonna miss the floor. Seems odd, I know, missing the floor. You see, not being on the floor means not being needed by him anymore. Not being on the floor means he doesn't need protection anymore; he's not walking on his own anymore. Means us not getting peed on anymore or stepped on in the middle of the night. Yet when you have a 'runner,' you do what you have to. Hubby and I had discussed it and decided that tying him down at night was out of the question, as was locking him in his bedroom. So at night we needed to know when he got out of the bed and left his room. We would lie next to his bed, on the floor, to know when he got out of the bed and started his roaming. He had to step over one of us or even on one of us before he could go anywhere else in the house. It's been a while since we slept on the floor, when I think about it. It's been a while…

I know I need to get up and get dressed. I know I do. Yet here I am…still counting those ceiling tiles and remembering. Wondering how this day is going to turn out. I've been listening for him to pull on the door, yelling to get out. Looking for keys. Crying from sadness. Wanting freedom again. Accepting that it just may not happen. Looking for something to eat. Looking for her.

I was standing at the kitchen sink that other day. He was watching me. I heard the front door open and close. Next thing I hear "BARBARA! BARBARA! BARBARA!" I am sure I started laughing inside cause whenever I hear *that* call, I smile. And I turn around and it's my baby boy. It's always good to see him. Where he ever got Barbara from is anybody's guess. My name doesn't look, sound or even rhyme with that name. Go figure. But I digress. As I said, he was watching me prepare food for dinner when the door opened. Next thing I know he's behind me, punching me in my side.

I tell you, dementia is horrible. You want to love, you want to help, you hope beyond hope that today will be better than yesterday (not for you but for them). You find yourself praying and believing, praying and hoping and, well, just praying. Illness will try you on every side. Especially as a caregiver. Illness will pull out of your darkest places stuff that has been lying hidden somewhere—those things you thought Jesus handled at salvation. Suddenly you realize that some things have laid in wait just to try to prove that salvation isn't your all in all. That's when you have to pull on your toolbox of love and stand firm in Jesus, knowing "It is finished!" Because truly, while you're getting hit on or peed on or cussed out or locked out, that inner man, the inner you, the one you thought had been transformed but now you're wondering if you had been, that one will show up. And the transformation you hoped for either happens at that very moment or all hell breaks loose. And it's not about you. So you have to keep reminding yourself what dementia is or what chemo does to the brain or how debilitating a stroke can be or how you would feel if you had to have two open heart surgeries with a stroke or a mastectomy at 75. And that this is not about you. That you're in this to win it. And that this has never been nor ever can be about you.

This time though, my son was there. He was always taking care of me. I mean always. I remember a time when we were driving to Virginia to visit family. He was still in his car seat, about three or four years old. It was just us (we did a lot together – just him and me). I took a wrong exit and wound up somewhere in DC, in a section that I had never been. It was about twilight. I could feel myself getting slightly nervous. This is the thing: He felt me getting nervous too, without me saying a single word. Next thing I know I hear this little voice say, "It's gonna be ok, Mommy." Funny thing, though—that little tiny voice was all I needed. I knew we would be ok. And we were.

As I said, dementia is horrible. So horrible things happen because of it. This bout of anger was nothing new. It was one of his ways of working out his frustration. He would get frustrated a lot. Mainly because he missed her. And he just couldn't understand why she didn't at least come to visit. 'Where did she go?' was a daily question. They had been together since he was 12 and she 11. His whole life, just about, had been about them. And now he was confused. He often thought I was her. I couldn't tell him the truth. Not again. I just couldn't. He never remembered so every time I told him where she was, he cried like it was the first time he heard it. His heart broke in front of me. He went through days of pain. Letting him think I was her was so much better than what I saw in his eyes every time he asked me to explain why she didn't come visit. Yet it was like walking a tightrope in the house, because he couldn't figure out why I was cheating on him in his home. Who was that man I was sleeping with? Hence…his frustration.

Yet I remember this particular time because my son happened to come by. I think it was the first time he had seen some of the unpleasant daily life experiences that we had progressed to. I remember telling Dad to stop. I remember going to my knees. I remember my son picking Daddy up and moving him to the other side of the kitchen. I remember him telling Daddy that he could never, ever, ever hit me like that again. I remember thinking, *It's gonna be ok, Mommy* and holding onto that memory. I remember God speaking quietly in my ear at that moment and saying 'Be patient. Let him have his freedom. It won't be long now.' By the fall of that year, he was no longer walking on his own. What I remember, though, most of all about that day, was what I 'heard' when I looked in my daddy's eyes. He didn't understand what was happening to him. It didn't make sense to him that his life had turned out like this. He was a Navy man who lived his life with order, who in the 1950s worked a full-time job all day and went to Temple at night to earn his degree. He was a true father in every sense of the word to his children and an amazing husband to his wife, as well as a provider for his mom, sisters and brother. He followed all the rules as best he could, while fighting every barrier in front of him to become an engineer when men of color just didn't do that. He planned his life out the way he believed you should. So none of this made any sense at all. He screamed this at me without saying a single word. I also saw how much he truly loved me, 'cause there's nothing like that daddy-daughter love. How sad he was for what had just happened. Eyes truly are the windows to the soul. That was the moment I learned to be careful when you look because the noise you see can be heart-wrenching. Suddenly you begin to realize that this thing is on you. You **have to** stop looking for others to show up and do. You **have to** stop looking for what doesn't exist. You **have to** stop judging by the actions you see (kick the enemy out of your head and love, no matter what). Suddenly you realize **_you_** have to submit to the process. Because until **_you_** do, **_you_** will be giving an opening, some type of false legality and fake truth to the cray-cray thoughts running around in **_your_** head. Believing that people do smell (sometimes) as badly as **_you_** think. Love them anyway. **_You_** will be constantly distracted by what **_you_** think they should be doing, losing **_your_** direction and purpose, forgetting **_your_** reason **_you_** said yes to begin with, unless you love them anyway. So I had to come to the conclusion that my 'yes' wasn't about them anyway. I mean, it is good that they are able to remain in their own homes, living life as they always have, without any real changes needed. Because my 'yes' was never theirs. My 'yes' was God's. Period.

Lying here, looking around this basement, I am reminded how I love, love, love to dance! And how, in the midst of so much stress, anxiety and rejection from those who were closest to me, God has a way of sending strength that only His joy can give. Not too long ago when I was standing at the kitchen sink, looking out of Mom's beautiful bay window, I was thinking about just how much I loved to dance. I remember this because it was early in the afternoon and I was thinking about how much I missed dancing with him. How I was about four when my real dance lessons began. You see, on Saturday mornings nobody went anywhere or did anything until their chores were done. NOBODY! In this house, if you could pick up a fork and feed yourself you had a chore. We learned at a very early age about love and all its parts...true love. That it not only involved true sacrifice but included things like honest earned respect. We were taught very young that when you take care of the things you own you will learn to appreciate them and to respect the process needed to keep them. If I heard it once, I heard it a thousand times: "Money don't grow on trees." "Don't play in your good clothes." "Take care of what you have." And as I got a little older, "Nobody stays anywhere for free." It was never a lot of chores or extremely hard chores or, when you started working at your first part-time after-school job, never much 'house' money you had to give. Yet it was just enough so we knew we were a family. That we were in this together. That it took a village for this to work and we were our own type of village right inside our house.

So I'd listen for it. The first couple times I missed it but it didn't take me long to begin to listen for it. He would make sure all my chores were finished, so Momma wouldn't get upset. And suddenly, just like that, in the twinkling of an eye, I would hear Harry Belafonte or the Ramsey Lewis Trio or Nina Simone playing from the basement. I listened because that was my signal. Soon as the music started flowing upward, before it could get a couple of good spins on the turntable, I was flying down those steps because I knew he was waiting with open arms to scoop me up and swing me around the floor. You see, Friday evenings usually were family time. Either the 61st Street drive-in (already in your pjs so when you got home, he would carry you upstairs and put you in your bed) or watching Dad hit golf balls at the driving range on 52nd & Parkside Avenue (and then running to gather them up so he could hit them again). Saturday evenings were party time most weekends. House party. Real house parties too. Uncles, aunts, cousins…dancing, drinking, uncle hiding food in the china closet only to forget it when he left (cause corn liquor will make you forget some things), having pinochle championships, eating Momma's fried chicken, potato salad, fresh biscuits, homemade dessert.

But just for a brief moment in time, Saturday mornings were ours. Just ours. All ours. And these are the memories that you hold onto. The bikes under the tree on Christmas mornings **or** the Christmas tree you and he picked up just the night before yet somehow Mom managed to transform into the bestest tree ever overnight **or** him protecting you from anything, anyone, everything. So as I was standing in the kitchen that day, looking at him watch me, I remember thinking at that moment, *Oh, how'd I'd love to dance with my daddy again.* Music was on the radio and so we did just that. The very last time I danced with my daddy. How sweet it was. Those memories are what holds you. Those memories are what makes you cry. Those memories are what keeps you and brings you past all the pain. Your poor decisions in life. Your lack of good judgment. None of it matters at this moment in time. He still loved you. He still held your hand. He danced with his daughter one last time. Only God!

As I lie here and reminisce about all those memories, it's then that I understand just how much they loved us. Just how much they cared. Just how much love can carry you—it truly does cover a multitude of sins. Love…no matter how splintered your heart may feel at times, there is nothing greater in life than love.

It was time for change. Yep. I could feel it in the wind. Not sure of what type of change but a change was coming. Shifting was happening. Too often now my back was hurting when we gave him his daily bath, or when we moved him to his chair (even with the hoist), or when we would take him for his doctor appointments. And truth be told, I'm tired a lot now. This never happened before. The seven years that I've been here I have never felt like this. I always felt like I could run this race and not get weary. Tired, sure. Weary, no. But now, it's the weariness that has had me concerned. God knew. He saw. He responded.

Lying here and counting these ceiling tiles, reminiscing, I see clearly that Life has challenged me over these seven years like nothing else. God knew. He saw. He responded. And if He did that for me then I can't be as useless and worthless as my mind thought and my heart believed! I realize that if He did that for me then who are they to have power and control over me?! I realize that now is the day and the time for me to take my eyes off people, regardless of the physical connections. "I am fearfully and wonderfully made; and I know it right well!" I choose my family and they will be the ones who do the will of my Father! I will apologize to all those who I may have offended in my life but my past is behind me. I have truly done my best to honor my mother and father. I have given it my all. God is pleased. And the rainbow is indeed enough! Yes, I will always remember January 9, 2010. It is the day I learned I am worthy to be loved!

Time to get up…I have work to do—a eulogy to give this morning. I'm excited!

Joanne McCrae is a quiet and humble woman with over 25 years of in-depth experience in highly responsible positions requiring practical interpersonal and communication skills. She is valued by many for her ability to analyze issues for resolutions by providing counseling skills and feedback that creates a positive outcome for those impacted by traumatic experiences.

Ms. McCrae has found her strength through having a relationship with God that put her on the path to healing and repairing all the broken pieces. Her faith has taught her the meaning of patience, knowing that good things come to those who wait and trust God.

Joanne's journey has strengthened her to walk by faith and not by sight, knowing that her son will be released from confinement and will return home just like Peter, one of Jesus' disciples in the bible.

Unfair Imprisonment of a Child

JOANNE MCCRAE

In 1989 I was an employee for First Union Bank, which merged with CoreStates Bank, and when I experienced a layoff in 2004, the bank merged again with Wachovia Bank in the Center City of Philadelphia. I worked fifteen years in the Research Adjustment Department, debiting and crediting other bank institutions and credit unions for internal accounting errors. I enjoyed working at the bank because it paid well, and I worked from 9 am to 5 pm on weekdays and every other weekend. Twice a month, my coworkers and I would go to the Phoenix Club on Arch Street in Center City of Philadelphia to unwind after work.

My life changed in 1995, when I had an incredible experience with God and accepted Jesus Christ as my Savior and joined Solomon Temple Baptist Church. I joined the adult usher board immediately after completing the new member class and being baptized. I had a zeal to learn about God by reading the Bible and being faithful to Sunday and midweek service. The hunger for God's word became so intense that I would come home from work, eat dinner, prepare for the next day, and sit at the kitchen table for hours reading the Bible and studying. Each pay period I would invest in purchasing different translations of the Bible, study Bibles and biblical dictionaries to build a library.

I became a first-time homeowner in 1997, so there would be something to pass down to the next generation. Things were looking good for the family; my son Lomar and my sister were attending high school in the Philadelphia area, and I was working at the bank. Everyone was happy. A year later, in 1998, Lomar received his first part-time job as a stock person at a supermarket in the Fairmount area of Philadelphia. Lomar was excited about working and helped with the household responsibilities, kept up with the latest fashion, and bought deer meat daily to feed his pit bull.

One evening after work, Lomar made a stop in North Philadelphia that changed his life and that of the family. There was a double homicide that occurred in Philadelphia, in the area Lomar had just left. The night of the incident, Lomar came home, and four days later, someone told him that the police were looking for him. Upon receiving the news, Lomar immediately said, "Mother, I did not do what they are saying" and began to pack some clothes. I began to cry and said, "What happened? What is going on?" I asked Lomar, "Where are you going?" Lomar responded, "Mother, I cannot stay here and go to jail for something I did not do" and left the house.

My nightmare began soon as Lomar gave me a hug and a kiss on the cheek as he closed the front door behind him. I quickly called my pastor, and he prayed for Lomar and me. I then called another clergy from the church, and she immediately began to pray. She said, "Sister Joanne, your son did not do what he is being accused of, and the truth will come out." I was told, "Sister Joanne, when you have a call on your life, believe it or not, it affects your children. Your child is not like the other children his age, simply because God made promises to you about yours." I said okay and hung up the phone but could not stop crying. I cried all night and went to work the next day. I had to go to work to save my paid time off days just in case I might need them to be there for Lomar.

One morning as I was preparing for work, there was a loud bang on the front door, and a voice said, "This is the police with a warrant; open up." I was so scared that I could not move for a moment. I walked downstairs to open the door, and the police and homicide detectives came in. They asked me questions about Lomar and if I was aware of the incident. I was handed a Philadelphia Police Department Wanted flyer with Lomar's picture and personal information, accusing him of a double homicide and saying he was considered armed and dangerous for a crime he did not commit. I closed the door behind them and screamed out to God, and said, "Please, please help me," knowing that I needed strength to go to work.

The homicide division returned two days later at 5:30 am. This time, they were rude and nasty. They were talking to me as if I had done something wrong. They came in and searched the entire house, upstairs and the basement, and left. The next day I noticed static in my telephone lines, followed by a marked car sitting on the block watching me. I felt like the walls were closing in on me, and I could not breathe, so I called out from work. I went to the movies at Andorra Shopping Center; as I was leaving the theatre, I locked eyes with a Caucasian man who was following me, hoping they would catch me meeting to see Lomar. I went to lunch and came back home to prepare for work.

Two days later, the dogs were barking in the backyard. My heart dropped, and I started crying and said, "Why are they doing this?" I looked out my bedroom window and saw police officers pointing their guns at the window. Then suddenly there was a loud bang. "Open up," demanded the police. Each time the authorities came, they were more aggressive toward me; one officer told me to sit down in a real nasty tone while they searched the house. Another officer said, "We are going to keep coming until you tell us where your son is." I never showed any tears in front of the police or the homicide division. There was a final encounter with the police and homicide division, and the Holy Spirit woke me up early to prepare for work. I had been praying to God for the nightmare to be over. One officer laughed and said, "We will be back," but this time I responded from within and said, "No, you will not." Months went by when I did not see or talk to Lomar, but he would send word: "Mother, I am okay. Keep your head up; we are going to get through this."

On January 10, 1999, Lomar surprised me and came to the Sunday service. My pastor interrupted service and asked Lomar and me to go to the front of the church. The pastor and the ministers prayed and anointed Lomar, and he left. Two days later, I received a phone call at 7:00 am saying, "Lomar was arrested" and the Holy Spirit immediately said, "I am starting the process." I did not go to work so that I could receive Lomar's phone call. He called and said, "Mother, I did not do anything; I will call you soon as I can; I love you." The next time I heard Lomar's voice, he said, "Mother, they are going to keep me and send me somewhere. I do not know where." My sister and I contacted a lawyer to explain everything and were scheduled to meet him with a deposit to start the process of representing Lomar.

In March of 2000, Lomar's court hearing began in the Commonwealth of Pennsylvania for double homicide. I had to be a character witness for my son and was cross-examined by the lawyer for the Commonwealth of Pennsylvania. It hurts so bad to hear people that neither you nor your child have seen before lying about him, but I could do nothing about it. The jury found Lomar guilty of first-degree murder, weapons possession, and conspiracy. On November 27, 2000, the lawyer told me he was going to appeal the court decision because he was not present when the Commonwealth of Pennsylvania and the judge cross-examined a witness who said Lomar was the shooter.

The court hearing would resume the next day to hear the penalty for the charges against Lomar. The Commonwealth of Pennsylvania determined that Lomar's sentence would be life in prison or capital punishment by lethal injection. The court verdict was on November 30, 2000; the jury found Lomar guilty of first-degree murder and sentenced him to lethal injection, 10- 20 years each for a firearm and conspiracy.

I was numb and shocked with disbelief because one witness described who they saw running with a firearm in their hand as the individual ran across the street. The individual was described as short and dark-skinned; Lomar is six feet and brown-skinned. The lawyer immediately grabbed my hand and said, "Ms. McCrae, I will appeal the Commonwealth of Pennsylvania's decision; do not worry". I watched the Commonwealth of Pennsylvania handcuff my son and escort him out of the courtroom. I went to court alone, and the victim's family was crying and said, "Now you will never see your son again." I felt so afraid for Lomar because he had never been arrested and did not know where the Commonwealth of Pennsylvania was taking him. The same night Lomar called and told me his location. Lomar sounded okay; his only concern was how I was doing. Lomar was angry because of the way I was cross-examined on the witness stand. He knew that the trial was not fair and he was keeping his faith and asked me to pray harder. The lawyer appealed the Commonwealth of Pennsylvania's decision, and the Supreme Court stated they did not find any errors in the case. When I heard Lomar's case was denied, the Holy Spirit said, "I will keep Lomar safe" because I had obeyed, and Lomar would not be punished for someone else's sin.

There was a second appeal issued with the Federal Court by a new attorney in December of 2004, because he felt Lomar was not accurately represented during the court hearing. Lomar was talked into signing papers to admit to a crime that he did not commit with a promise to be released but was instead charged for two murders and sent directly to a correctional facility. The same judge that sentenced Lomar at the first court hearing would hear the case again and I was sad because it hurt so bad, like hitting a healing sore. The second appeal was called the PCRA Post Conviction Release Act and would take a couple of years before Lomar would receive a response.

The Pennsylvania governor signed a warrant for the death penalty on January 11, 2005. One evening, my son called me and said, "Mother, I am about to tell you something. I want to prepare you. I am scheduled for execution, and you will receive my death certificate in the mail. I want you to know, Mother, that I love you," and we hung up the phone. A mother's desire is that their child has the best of life with equal opportunities to make a difference in the world. No parent wants to lose a child to death under any circumstances. So when I heard "Mother, you will receive a death certificate in the mail," my first response was, *How am I going to make it without my son?*

I screamed so loud and slid down the kitchen wall and fell on the floor. It felt like I was on the floor for hours, crying and praying to God. The very next day, the new attorney called and explained everything to me; he stated "Lomar wanted to be the one to tell you about the death warrant. I am calling to tell you that an execution warrant was signed today, January 13, 2005. The judge signed a stay order, which means Lomar may get a life sentence instead of the death penalty." When I hung up the phone with the attorney I said, "Not so, Lomar is innocent, and the truth will come out because we trust God." The Holy Spirit told me on March 28, 2006, "I will send him home, and restored. I am working on it. You will win if you don't quit." In 2013, the Pennsylvania General Assembly wanted to change legislation of life sentences to "Parole Eligibility" for life sentences after 25 years. At the time, Lomar had served 14 years and was not eligible for parole.

I kept holding on to the words that were spoken: "Lomar did not do it," and "the truth will come out." The trial lasted for two weeks and I left the courtroom crying, trying to understand what just happened. I know what God told me: Lomar was innocent and the truth would come out. I had in my mind that the truth was going to come out during the trial, and when it did not, I was devastated. I would go to work and come home to prepare for the next day and then go to bed. I fell into depression and felt myself slipping deeper, and God rescued me. I was not talking to anyone or eating, and my job was in jeopardy because I had exhausted my paid leave. One evening God used my niece to bring me out of my depression; she began telling jokes that made me laugh. I remained faithful to God and never stopped serving Him and continued ushering, then became involved with the youth department. The more I studied the Bible, I found myself praying for the families that lost their son and the first attorney who didn't represent Lomar with confidence in his innocence.

Staying busy in the church helped me to get through my adversity by spending time with the youth. I was selected to be the leader of the youth department, including the junior usher board. I kept pushing and believing God's promise that Lomar would return home. As I was serving God, people were astounded and would ask me, "How are you working with children and your son incarcerated?" I became a mentor to the female teenagers in my community and a team leader at an after-school program. I tried to live a holistic life by dating during my separation from Lomar.

Unfortunately, that experience turned out to be horrible; I could never celebrate a second anniversary because they were unfaithful relationships. I did not have any luck dating, so I began dating and loving myself to discover that it was a challenge to learn who I was in the eyes of God. Often, I thought that it was good that the relationships did not lead to marriage. I would not want Lomar to feel that his mother had moved on with her life without him.

As a queen who defied the odds while her only child was incarcerated, I ensured the family remained focused on God. I was able to walk out my destiny that God had planned for me to be a kingdom builder. I received two college degrees in early childhood education, am an author of a book titled *Learning to Love Me While Putting the Pieces Back Together*, and am a licensed minister for the gospel of Jesus Christ. I am also a certified facilitator for pre-married and married couples and an entrepreneur for "We Have A Voice, Inc.," mentor program for young ladies aged 10 to 20 years old. While working on becoming a mental health coach, I continue to hold on to the words, "Lomar is innocent, and the truth will come out."

In this long process, we know that God's timing is perfect according to Psalms 31:15, KJV: *"My times are in thy hand; deliver me from the hand of mine enemies, and from them that persecute me."* I have learned that God's timing is different from Lomar's or my timing. As I mentioned earlier, I had expected the truth to come out during the two weeks of the trial. It was not easy for Lomar and the family to adjust to the separation. I had to be mindful and not cry when I visited Lomar at the correctional facility or when leaving. The first time I cried Lomar said, "Mother, stop crying because you must be strong for the both of us."

We could see that God was bringing Lomar home soon because it was originally an eight-hour drive to visit him. The driving time had gotten shorter, to six and a half hours, and now it is a forty-five-minute drive. Once the COVID 19 restriction is lifted, the family will take advantage of the visitation policies and see Lomar daily.

I have learned that God is not like man and will not lie to me; according to Numbers 23:19, NKJV, *"God is not a man, that He should lie, Nor a son of man that He should repent. Has He said, and will He not do? Or has He spoken, and will He not make it good?"* I can see the evidence of Lomar returning home to his family. I learned how to pray and trust God as I strived to beat the odds concerning Lomar and for my peace of mind. I now understand the revelation of Deuteronomy 31: 6, NKJV *"Be strong and of good courage, do not fear nor be afraid of them; for the Lord your God, He is the One who goes with you. He will not leave you nor forsake you."* My God was with us from the very beginning of the process.

Currently, Lomar is waiting for the parole board to review his petition to meet for a release date. In the meantime, he used his time wisely by completing certifications like high school diploma, victim awareness, drug and alcohol outpatients, money smarts, a pathway to success, business/technology, and is now working on the introductory classes to become an entrepreneur. The set-apart experience produced fruit in Lomar mentally, emotionally, and spiritually to desire to help others who were falsely accused of a crime to unite with their families.

Jane Victoria Hopkins is a child of God and has been on an unbelievable journey for God. Her favorite Scriptures are Jeremiah 29:11 and Isaiah 61:1-3. She received her Bachelor's degree in Business Administration from Pierce College in 2004 and her Master's Degree in Christian Studies: Christian Leadership from Grand Canyon University in 2011. She obtained a Bachelor's degree in Biblical Studies from Lancaster Bible College in 2021.

Jane is a dedicated member of the Christian Hope Baptist Church where Stephen W. Howard is the Pastor. She has been a member for 38 years. She is a Deaconess and the Assistant Superintendent of Sunday School. Jane is also a dedicated teacher of the Adult Sunday School. She is an active participant of WOW (Women of Wellness) and attends many of their workshops, seminars, and conferences.

Jane currently lives in Philadelphia and she enjoys the great outdoors, cooking, traveling, reading, and networking.

Surviving a Coma and Thriving

JANE VICTORIA HOPKINS

Hi, I am Jane Victoria. I am 66 years old, and this is my first attempt at writing about myself. I am here to tell you a story about my recovery from pneumonia and subsequent coma that I had some eight years ago. But first, I want to share with you a little about myself and who I am. My parents are the late Lemon DeWitt Hopkins and Lillian P. Jenkins. My father is Bahamian, from the Island of the West Indies and my mother was born in Sumter, South Carolina and was the great-granddaughter of a former slave. I am one of seven children. My brothers, Moses, Nathaniel, and Roosevelt, along with my sister Betty Jean, have gone home to be with the Lord. My brother DeWitt and my sister Hilda and their children are the only family I have left. People have said that I am more like my father: strong, determined, and confident. Others say I take on my mother's traits: compassionate, kind, loving to a fault, and always caring for others before herself. Because of who my father and mother are and what they meant to me, I have tried all my life to live in a way that honors them and their spirit of caring and giving.

I am a graduate of William Penn High School (formerly Yeadon High School), located in Yeadon, Pa. I currently hold degrees from the following colleges: 1) Associate's Degree in Business from

Delaware County Community College, 2) Bachelor's Degree in Business Administration from Pierce College, 3) Master's Degree from Grand Canyon University in Christian Leadership-Worship. I was an Administrative Assistant for several years for several different corporate businesses, but due to numerous health issues and the inability to work full-time, I retired from the work force in 2005. I have been a member of the Christian Hope Baptist Church for 38 years and served on several ministries. I currently serve as Deaconess on the Deaconess Ministry and hold the position of secretary. I am a resident of Philadelphia. I am single and I have no children. I love the outdoors, watching professional sports—in particular professional football and basketball—traveling, walks (in my power wheelchair), dining out, reading, writing in my journals, and meditating. So, you now know a little something about me. Now I want to share with you about a major medical condition I suffered.

It was a warm evening, and I was sitting outside listening to some of my favorite gospel music on my phone when one of my favorite gospel artists, Marvin Sapp came on. The song that was played was "My Testimony." I thought to myself as I was listening to the song how fitting considering how far I had come. Who would have thought that nearly eight years ago, I would be hospitalized with what I thought was a simple case of pneumonia, but turned out to be much more serious? I slipped into a coma after suffering a seizure/stroke. I lay there in that hospital bed for two weeks or more, not knowing if I would live or die, let alone wake up from what I considered a nightmare. I could not tell day from night or vice versa. I did not recognize any of my surroundings. I was confused and fearful. Believing I was not going to wake up, I lay there in that coma and visualized my own funeral. There I was, laid out in a white casket, dressed in white from head to toe. Flowers were everywhere; my brother and sister, along with a host of nieces and nephews, were sitting there crying.

Mourners were there, some of whom I recognized and some I did not. What an awful feeling. The whole scene seemed unreal. But I serve a merciful God. He woke me up. That's why I can sing, "I am so glad I made it. He brought me through." God had a plan for me, and it was not my time.

All this happened on the heels of my brother Moses passing away. Here I was dealing with two major life crises at the same time. But I am reminded that there is power in the name of Jesus, healing power, comforting power in times of hardship and struggle. Only he has the power to break the chains that were binding me. That is when I knew I needed to fight back. So once my doctors had stabilized my condition and built up my strength, I was transferred to a rehabilitation center. There is where the work began to get me walking again, teaching me how to dress myself, wash myself, and feed myself. I also had some difficulty with my speech, so I had to undergo speech therapy. It was extremely hard work and some days I felt like I would not make it. If you were to ask me what the hardest part of rehabilitation was, I would have to say learning to walk, putting one foot in front of the other. Standing and maintaining balance came in a close second.

The one thing rehabilitation did not help me with was the emotional side of all of this. The highs and lows, the feelings of being lost and the feelings of abandonment were profound for me. I also experienced the feelings of being forgotten and that no one would remember me or visit me while I was in rehab. I had no clue as to what to expect next. Then it came to me that I needed a gentle reminder. And that reminder came to me in the form of Jesus speaking to me. He touched me gently on the shoulders and said, "Fear not, for I am with you; be not dismayed, for I am your God; I will strengthen you, I will help you, I will uphold you with my righteous right hand" (Isaiah 41:10 ESV). He told me to have faith and courage, "for I have plans for you" (Jeremiah 29:11). What these plans were, I did not immediately know. All I did know was that I had to get ready for whatever those plans were. And get ready I did. I got up every single day and went down to the rehab room. I worked hard and pushed myself as hard as I could at every exercise they asked me to perform. I successfully completed rehab and was discharged. My new life and journey were about to begin. I moved into a new apartment and set up housekeeping once more. Of course, when I was discharged, I was given tools, contacts, and phone numbers to help me along. The state provided me with a caregiver who came three times a week to help me get showered and dressed and assisted me in making my breakfast and performed other household duties.

Of course, I had to maintain all my doctor's appointments, along with any additional rehab I might have needed. I even started going to church on a regular basis. Since my whole life was built on being a faithful Christian and a member of the body of Christ, I knew that was where I needed to be. In church I could start teaching again and share my testimony of surviving the coma that nearly took my life. Remember when I said that God had a plan for me? Well, that plan was finally revealed to me. God came to me one night, as he does most every night, and said to me, "I want you to return to school. This will be the next step in your journey. There you will learn and gain a deeper meaning of what I am all about." Now, I have learned never to ignore or question God when he tells or directs you to do something. You obey. After much prayer and talking with God and on the recommendation of a close friend, I applied to Lancaster Bible College for the Winter term, beginning January 2020, and was accepted. Glory!!! The course of study recommended to me by the Enrollment Advisor was the Biblical Studies program. This field of study was an accelerated degree program with a new class beginning every six weeks.

So I knew this was not going to be easy for me, because I was still learning to be on my own, but I made a commitment and knowing that God was in my corner and walking right beside me, I jumped in feet first and started this journey to success. Finally, after approximately 18 months of reading chapter after chapter of textbooks, research on the school's library site, and writing tons of papers, I will be graduating from Lancaster Bible College with a Bachelor of Arts degree in Biblical Studies. I am so excited and thrilled that I have successfully reached this milestone in my life despite all that I had been through and the minor setbacks. So you see, you can thrive and grow. What a wonderful achievement for me as well as for anyone who thinks that because of their disability or medical condition they cannot succeed as I did. I am living proof that you can. There were times, though, I could have quit and given up, but I did not. The long nights of studying, reading, and writing papers into the wee hours of the morning were more than I could bear sometimes. I also had to take time away from this to keep up with my doctor's appointments. That meant I would lose whole days and by the time I got home from the appointments, I would be so tired and hungry all I wanted to do was go eat and go to sleep. And most of the time, that is what I did. Instead of waiting for the next day, I would get up in the middle of the night to write a paper or read a chapter. That is how dedicated and determined I was to succeed.

But I persevered and now I have come to the end of one journey. What is next for me, you ask? Well, I am going to take a break, catch up on some rest, and take a few day trips. I especially want to visit the African American Museum as well as the Philadelphia Museum of Art. I want to experience and enjoy life now that I am more mobile and independent. My 67th birthday is in September. It would be wonderful if I could go away for the weekend somewhere that is completely handicap-accessible, where I could relax in the sun, eat, shop, and enjoy life. I will also be taking some time to consider the possibility of going into seminary to study Theology or continue my learning in Biblical Studies and obtaining a Master's degree. I have already begun to do some preliminary research on which seminary schools are the best and whether they offer 100% online programs. There are a few excellent seminaries out there. I am confident I will find a seminary that fits my needs. I am also extremely excited about some projects that I have been asked to work on. I am also hoping to start my own blog page, where I can reach out to those who, like myself, live with a disability or have experienced a serious medical condition, to have a place to post and share their feelings without feeling they're less than human.

What I want most for people to get from reading about my experience and my survival and recovery is that I did not let it keep me down. I did not let the naysayers distract me or steal my joy. I took control of my life. I also took advantage of every opportunity to stay involved and be socially active as much as I could. I tell myself every day that I have been blessed. God gave me a second chance at life. Be grateful for the small things and serve others with joy and gladness. I could have given up on myself and stayed in the shell that I had created. But I realized that was not what I wanted, and neither did God. He wanted me to live and thrive and enjoy life. But most importantly, he wanted me to continue to serve him and spread the gospel. So now I travel around the city in my motorized wheelchair, enjoying life. I attend Church every Sunday, and I go out to lunch with friends. I am free of the shame of being disabled because there is no shame in being disabled. I am still a person, a human being. I am a woman who is living with a disability and even more important, I survived a coma. I am thriving and I am achieving new goals every day. I am a beautiful black woman. I live each day with passion and excitement. I look forward to each new day with anticipation of what's to come. And when I talk with God, he is pleased with me and excited for me. If I learned anything in this life, I learned you must have a personal relationship with God, because when things get tough, and they do, you need someone to turn to. God is an excellent listener, and his advice and guidance never fails but you must be willing to accept it and follow him.

I want to take a moment to say a few words about faith. Hebrews 11:1 ESV says, "Now faith is the assurance of things hoped for, the conviction of things not seen." Max Lucado says, "Meet your fears with faith." The Rev. Dr. Martin Luther King, Jr., said, "Faith is taking the first steps even when you do not see the whole staircase." Faith is defined as complete trust or confidence in someone or something, and when it comes to religion, faith is one of the cornerstones of your personal relationship and your spirituality. Having faith can make your connection with the Lord stronger. God is always watching over you, in good times and in bad.

God was certainly watching over me while I lay there in the hospital in a coma. He kept me safe from all harm and guided the doctors and nurses as they cared for me. If it had not been for the Lord on my side, where would I be?" Always remember that the true meaning of faith is belief, firm persuasion, assurance, firm conviction, faithfulness. Faith knows that no matter what the situation, in our lives or someone else's, the Lord is working in it. Real faith is more than just believing in God alone. It includes acting on that faith in one's life by serving God and obeying His commandments. In Ephesians 2:8-9, NKJV Paul writes, "For by grace you have been saved through faith; and that not of yourselves; it is the gift of God, not of works, lest anyone should boast." My faith in God was as strong, if not stronger, before I got sick and increased even more as I lay there in a coma. I had faith the size of a mustard seed. It continued to grow in immense proportions, making me stronger with each passing day of my recovery. There was no doubt in my mind that the Lord's hand was at work. I never gave up hope and I would not let any of my family give up on me either. You might say that I have a mustard seed, and I am not afraid to use it.

Faith is increased by drawing closer to God through prayer and the study of His Word, the Bible. In trying times, I needed God's love and spirit and guidance to get me through. I could not go it alone. I needed him during my rehabilitation, and I still need him now. My recovery was nothing short of a miracle, a miracle that only God could have performed. Living faith is accomplished by service and obedience to God and His laws (Romans 3:31). By keeping my faith in God and my mind stayed on him, I have a positive attitude and I can reflect on his promises. Praising Jesus in all things and in all circumstances means I can surrender my circumstances to Him. I can ask him to help me change my circumstances. I just need to let Him take the wheel and trust what He is going to do. In other words, I need to get out of God's way and let him do his works. Spending more time in his Word helped keep me grounded and not going in another direction due to being confused or desperate.

So, my Queens, never give up on your dreams, never compromise or settle for less than what you deserve. Always pursue your desires. Never let your being handicapped or your disability stop you from achieving or reaching that high calling. Philippians 3:14, KJV reads, "I press toward the mark for the prize of the high calling of God in Christ Jesus." Whenever there is a challenge facing you, you must learn how to press on. I have faced many challenges and continue to do so every day, but I trust God, and I continue to press on no matter what those challenges are. So no looking back on what could have been, do not give up, keep on pressing, keep on striving because the goal is to cross the finish line. Most importantly, take the Lord with you. No matter what we try to do in life, we need the Lord. Yolanda Adams sings it best: "Never Give Up."

Rev. Beverly Gray is the Founder/Organizer of The Balm in Gilead Domestic Violence Intervention Ministry. She equips/certifies, Pastors, clergy, laypersons & community leaders to become advocates of Domestic/Intimate Partner Abuse. She organizes/facilitates City Wide DV Symposiums, Women in Ministry Conferences/Retreats and Youth DV Conferences at Community Colleges, Hotel Conference Centers, and various churches.

Rev. Beverly Gray is an ordained minister and Pastor. She was President of the PBEKA Women's Ministry 2016. She is a proud member of Zeta Phi Beta Sorority Inc, Beta Delta Zeta Chapter. She earned a Master of Human Services and MBA Degree from Lincoln University. She received her Chaplain Diploma from Palmer Theological Seminary and is currently a candidate for a PHD/Doctor of Management degree, Thomas Jefferson University.

Beverly is currently a Program Director of a homeless program. She has more than 30 years of experience in the social service field between NYC & Philadelphia, PA including SELF, Inc, Women Against Abuse, Project Home and the Philadelphia Criminal Justice Center.

I Win in the End

REVEREND BEVERLY GRAY

When life is good, enjoy it. But when life is hard, remember, God gives good times and hard times, and no one knows what tomorrow will bring.
~ Ecclesiastes 7:14 (NCV)

"Who is she?" I asked as soon as my husband walked into the bedroom.

He didn't know I was staring out the window when an unfamiliar car stopped in front of our home. I had a good look at the driver of the car. It was after 10:00 pm, but the driver's long curly hair and sparkling earrings gave away her identity.

"Who is she?" I asked again with more force.

He stared at me with his beady eyes and I could see the rage building quickly. I used to love looking into his eyes. They had a way of making me feel special ... and loved. But for several years now, all I felt when our eyes met was pain. And pain was what was about to follow tonight. But I didn't care. I had had enough.

I parted my lips to speak again, but before I could say another word, he threw me into the closet. As I tried to regain my balance, he grabbed me and pushed me into the dresser so hard that it broke. I was used to the physical abuse, but tonight was different. I was tired. Tired of living a lie. Tired of my neighbor asking if everything was okay. Tired of disappointing my kids. And tired of letting God down.

So I let him finish the thrashing and verbal abuse. When he was done, I sat on the floor, crippled in my brokenness. Weeping in silence, I watched him undress, walk to the bathroom to shower, and then return to crawl into the bed we shared. As he began to snore, I pulled my knees tighter to my chest and told myself it was time to go. This had gone on far too long.

· · · · · · ·

This is a difficult story to tell, but one that is needed to share in this season.

It was easy to fall in love with my husband. He was kind, he was a sharp dresser, and his accent was intriguing. It also didn't hurt that he was so nice to look at. At the time we met, I was a widow and a mother to two children. I was a minister and served on a number of ministries and boards because I was passionate about helping those in need.

The day he walked into my church, he caught everyone's attention with his style. He was well versed in the Bible and boy, could he pray. Although I was a widow, the last thing on my mind was starting a relationship with someone new. But I couldn't deny how attractive and kind he was. I thought he would be a great husband for someone other than me in the congregation someday. In those days, I didn't recognize my own beauty. Growing up, I was often ridiculed for my looks. I was lighter than most of the people in my environment and I had what they called "good hair." I was often told that I was attractive and had a great shape, but it was not a compliment to me because I did not see it. I was given the nickname "Baby Doll" by my grandfather and "White Girl" by everyone else, because of my skin tone and hair texture. Growing up this way led to a number of insecurities, but I didn't let it show. I was often spicy with my speech and tolerated very little nonsense.

Eventually this nice guy became a member of my church, and I hadn't realized it, but he had started courting me. He paid attention to me and showered me with compliments all the time. He opened doors and pulled out my chair at tables. If I walked into the church with packages, he would gently relieve me of them and escort me to my destination. In my eyes, he was a great man, so when he asked me on a date, I accepted the invitation. After all, I was lonely, and he was a good Christian man serving the Lord. I had no reason to believe I was being set up.

For our first date, he took me to City Island in New York. We enjoyed a great meal at Sammy's Fish Box Restaurant, and an even better conversation. He treated me like a Queen and paid for everything! This was the beginning of a beautiful romance. We talked every day, sometimes three times a day. There were very few moments when we were not together. If I drove to pick up a friend, he would ride with me. If I went to the grocery store, he wanted to know what time I would be back home. He said he loved being around me and I soaked up all the attention like a sponge. It felt good to have someone like me ... I mean *really* like me, all of me, just the way I was.

My children didn't share in my enthusiasm, but this was the first man they had seen me with since their father died in a car accident. I figured they would get to know him over time. He was so kind and accommodating to me, I couldn't imagine that he would be anything less to my children. It was no secret that we were a package deal.

The romance continued and my life was blossoming. I was appointed to pastor my second church and receiving more preaching engagements. This called for me to travel more doing ministry. One day, as I was preparing for one of my services, he informed me that he was called to preach as well and was talking to our pastor about this. I was overjoyed. Not only had God blessed my life with someone special, but God also blessed me with a man who loved to share the Good News with God's people just as much as I did. Life couldn't get any better than this.

About eighteen months into our relationship, he told me to dress up for a special dinner. I was so excited. I made sure my hair and nails looked perfect. We were just going to another couple's home, but I wanted to look good for my man. And I did.

The dinner went well and then just like a scene out of a blockbuster movie, the woman of the house brought out dessert accompanied with champagne-filled glasses. As I sipped on my glass, something hard fell into my mouth. Lo and behold, it was a ring. I pulled the ring from my mouth and looked at my man, who was now on bended knee. "Will you marry me?" he asked.

His eyes were so warm and inviting—how could I say no? Even though in my heart I knew I wasn't ready, I couldn't say no. I didn't want to embarrass him in front of these nice church members, so I lovingly stared back into his eyes and smiled. "Yes," I replied. "I will marry you."

Planning the wedding happened too quickly. Everyone in the church, especially the pastor, was excited for our union. My family was a little concerned that things were moving too fast, but they supported me. I began looking for the perfect dress. My sister went out shopping to find the dress of my dream. I called my man to share my shopping experience, only to find that he went out and found a dress *for* me, along with the headpiece. I was a little taken aback at this. It did bother me that he saw the dress before Daddy had a chance to walk me down the aisle in it, but I just went along with it. This should have been a red flag, a sign that something was not right.

On the morning of the wedding, I went to the salon, and he was right by my side. I excitedly described the style I wanted. "Can you give me a French Roll with dangling curls going down one side?"

Immediately, he responded, "Give her lots of curls."

"That's not how *I* want *my* hair," I said firmly. But after a few smooth words, I gave in to his request.

Despite the curly hair, our wedding was beautiful. So was the honeymoon. We decided to move into his tiny apartment while we searched for a new home together. Although I had a bigger home, I was taught to "follow the man." I didn't like that my children had to sleep on the floor, but I convinced them that it was temporary. "Our next home will be much larger than this and your bedrooms will be huge," I'd say every time they complained. We never did move into a big house, and looking back, I believe that moving was never in his plan.

Well before we moved into the house, we moved into a two-bedroom apartment in the projects. All three kids shared the room. My two had a bunk bed and his had a daybed. We stayed there for a year then we finally moved into the house. It was a nice house.

It didn't take long after the wedding for our "good" life to change. For as much as he was loving and caring, he was also mean and ornery.

Too often I found myself walking on eggshells in our home to avoid hurting his feelings.

It didn't matter that we were both preaching and loved the Lord. The arguments between us seemed to increase with each new month, as did the physical abuse. Numerous times I showed up in church after wrestling with his devilish ways. Countless times I sat in church wearing an invisible mask. No matter how intense our disagreements were, I showed up in church with a happy "I love Jesus" face.

But even in my sadness, I pressed my way to church. I had to continue to help and inspire others. Preparing sermons saved me, and preaching kept me grounded. These were constant reminders that I was not alone. God was with me, and His Holy spirit was keeping me safe. But there were also times that I struggled to hear from God and to stay focused, especially when I knew my husband was on his way home. There were many times that I thought I would not make it, but God! I constantly prayed for my situation to change. I preached with power in hopes that God would feel my turmoil and change my husband's heart. But week after week, things stayed the same. However, the Holy Spirit wouldn't let me give up on myself or on God. So I prayed that God would give me a message to share that would bring joy and encouragement to the congregation. It was important to me that they were able to hear from God, even if I could not.

Women would come up to me regularly to let me know how lucky I was to have married my husband. "He's such a nice guy," they would say. "I wish I had a husband like that."

Under my breath, I would mumble, "Be careful what you wish for." They didn't know about his violent streak or about the time he pushed me down a flight of stairs. They didn't know about all the secrets in the pulpit. And there was no one I could tell. We were both well-respected preachers. I was afraid and too embarrassed to confide in anyone about my situation. I couldn't take the chance that they would keep my secret, and I especially didn't want to be judged. I tried talking to my spiritual leader at the time. I'll never forget his response.

"What did you do to make him act this way?" he questioned.

I was stunned. How could anyone justify a man putting his hands on a woman? Especially if that man was an ordained minister. God teaches us to love one another. There is no love in domestic abuse. Women must know that there is nothing they could ever do that would give a man the right to be abusive: mentally, physically, or emotionally.

I remained in the marriage for seven years. Seven years. That's a long time. I was alone and isolated from family and friends. I'll never forgive him, or myself, for missing the 80th birthday celebration of my grandmother. That woman raised me. I'll never get that moment back. But at the time, I was more afraid of what he would do to me when I returned from the celebration than about missing such a special occasion for someone that I loved dearly.

So the night he came home late, after being with another woman, I thought of all the pain I had endured throughout the years. That night, after his anger bruised my mind and my body, I vowed to do what was needed to get me and my children away from his grip. It was time for change. If my son saw the bruises or found out how the dresser was broken, I would be visiting him in the penitentiary. There was no way I was going to ruin my son's life because I was afraid and ashamed to leave. So as I watched him sleep peacefully that night, I came up with a plan. It was important that this transition be safe and secure for my family.

God blessed me with a landlord who cared about my wellbeing and the wellbeing of my children. Things were so bad that she allowed me to save half of the rent so I could move into a place quickly. The place I found was very small and full of mold. I ended up getting bronchitis and bad migraines, so we had to move again. We moved so much after leaving that apartment that we were eventually homeless. But I refused to go back to my husband.

Besides, what would I be going back to? I had no doubt that his behavior would be worse toward me and my children if I returned. It was bad enough that he pretended our separation was a mutual decision. In church he would say hello with that deceiving smile and ask, "How are you?" His efforts led the congregation to believe that I had done something wrong in the marriage. They didn't know that the kids and I never knew where we would lay our heads at night. We were surviving the best way we could. And yes, I was *still* preaching. Somehow God gave me the strength to deliver messages of love, hope, and encouragement. From the pulpit, no one could see that I was dying inside. They couldn't see that I was ashamed, heartbroken, and disgusted.

Needless to say, going to church became very uncomfortable. It was difficult for me to hear from God and even harder to listen to my husband deliver the Word. How was he able to stand before God's people knowing that he crushed my spirit and abused me? I couldn't stand to see or hear him laughing with other people, especially other women. It's amazing how so many women flocked to him so easily, knowing we hadn't officially divorced. *If only they knew the truth,* I'd say.

I eventually decided to leave New York and head to Philadelphia. My mother lived there, and I needed her love and support. The apartment that we were living in was making us all sick and I couldn't bear living there anymore. Something had to change. Life began to change once we relocated. My mother found us a beautiful two-bedroom apartment. Finally, my children and I were able to rest at night in peace. Even though I drove my daughter to and from school in New York for four months until the school year finished, I was slowly beginning to regain control of my life and flush my husband out of my system once and for all. After losing so much time and so much of myself, I was ready to rebuild. I was ready to win.

Life was still a rollercoaster ride, but God gave me the strength to deal with it one day at a time. I couldn't see what was ahead, but God knew the future He had planned for me. God opened a door for me and I landed a good job at the courthouse. Then I had an opportunity to work with domestic violence victims. I started out as an on-call Resident Advisor and quickly moved up the ranks to a full-time Resident Advisor. While employed there, my friend who was a case manager told me about a program at Lincoln University. I was nervous, but I had to apply. I had started college when I was with my husband, but he complained that I wasn't home enough, so I dropped out. Now that he was no longer in the picture, I had to prove to myself that I could earn a degree. And I did. I earned Bachelor's and Master's degrees in Human Services. From there I accepted a position as a case manager for women against abuse. I continued to grow, thrive and win! I went to Palmer Seminary for my chaplain diploma because I wanted to be equipped to help others.

I was finally winning in life, and I was able to hear clearly from God. He told me that one day my mess would be my ministry. My soul would be healed through my ministry and so would the souls of numerous women. I just needed to step out on faith. So I did. With the encouragement of Sister Pauline Moore, I shared my story to a group of women at Tenth Memorial Baptist Church. As a result, I started a ministry at that church called *Balm in Gilead*. Through this ministry I was able to educate pastors, clergy, and members of the community on how to be an advocate for people dealing with domestic violence. Soon I was teaching and developing training seminars in various schools. My passion for helping others in this area grew stronger as the years passed. I decided to go back to school. This time I earned an MBA and was accepted in the Doctorate in Management program at Thomas Jefferson University! Look at God!

I went from being a victim of abuse, being homeless and jobless, to being the Director of a homeless program and a candidate for a PhD. I may have gone through turmoil and pain to get here, but God blessed me to win in the end. I have survived it all. I am a Conqueror,

And guess what? The best is still yet to come! I win in the end!

Renai Ellison is a Non-Profit Leader and Leadership Development Coach / Consultant who began her career as a television personality. She currently serves as Interim Executive Director for a non-profit organization where she began as a Reconciliation Consultant. In her immediate past position, Renai worked full-time as a Consultant and offered coaching, training, consulting, and instructional design services. Renai's dedication and training as a leader has afforded her opportunities to work as an Executive Coach and trainer for leaders at BMW of North America and the New York Department of Citywide Administrative Services. She also coached and facilitated training programs for physicians and other medical professionals at healthcare organizations.

After a stint as a Show Host on QVC, she created a clothing line on QVC and then co-hosted a home décor and craft series on HGTV called "Our Place." Renai hosted "For Women Only", a live, medical, call-in show on WPSJ-TV. She embarked on national media tours and appeared on countless morning shows across the country. Often serving as Fundraising Host for New Jersey Network (NJN) Public Television, Renai hosted national PBS fundraising shows.

For 14 years, Renai served as Mistress of Ceremonies for the New Jersey Lottery on NJN and has made personal appearances for the lottery throughout the state of New Jersey. Renai executive produced and hosted Embrace Life with Renai, a human-interest television program sponsored by a healthcare system, which aired on WMCN in the Philadelphia regional market. She also hosted Joy in Our Town, a public affairs television show featured on Trinity Broadcasting Network (TBN) and served as a reporter/host for Better Philly, a women's magazine show, on My PHL17 in Philadelphia. She is currently the host of YOUR DELAWARE on DeTV.

A School Called Life

RENAI ELLISON, Ed.D.

He winked at me. An overwhelming feeling of excitement and self-assuredness washed over me. *You got this!* I knew I was doing a good job. I drove for 45 minutes to that television studio with the music blasting while praying to God for the desires of my heart. I had arrived at a place in my life where my hard work was finally paying off. This was my very first audition after taking acting lessons for six months. I was about to land the job of my dreams. After spending my entire childhood and adulthood sitting in front of a television, I was about to *be* on television. I was about to become the person inside the box that I had obsessed over for decades. From soap operas to game shows to nighttime comedies and dramas to PBS documentaries to home shopping to the Oprah Winfrey Show, I watched it all. Now, after struggling to find my voice, I was ready to be watched. Here comes Renai Ellison! My heart leaped out of my chest with excitement as I described and sold the most obscure product on camera. I was bubbly. I was enthusiastic. I was passionate. As Les Brown would say, "I was hungry!" And I nailed it!

Several weeks later, I was mired in concern and worry because I hadn't heard anything. I picked up the phone to call the person who asked me to audition. She answered the phone. We exchanged pleasantries and then she said, "Why haven't you expressed an interest before this, Renai? Your audition was outstanding." I knew at that moment my life would never be the same...and it wasn't. After modeling on the show for nearly two years, I was hired to be a show host on a popular television shopping network. International television. The chubby kid who grew up on a South Jersey farm was about to embark on the ride of her life.

This wasn't the first time in my life that I surpassed expectations. It was similar to when I won student government president in high school, or when I won homecoming queen in college. I was the first black to do both. However, this was the opportunity of a lifetime... one for which I dreamed and prepared. At 26 years old, I felt I had reached the pinnacle of my career. I honestly thought this opportunity was my Mary Tyler Moore moment. I was metaphorically tossing my hat in the air and I truly thought I would make it after all. My prayer aligned with God's plan and my moment was about to come to fruition. Then reality set in. True colors began to surface, and the bloom faded from the rose.

Being on television came easy to me. I loved talking to viewers and doing fashion and home presentations. Selling those pesky tech products and silly gadgets did not come easy to me. I fell flat on my face and had a hard time connecting to the audience when selling those items. To "support" my struggling skill level, I was given hour-long technology shows with everything from air purifiers to computers to blood pressure monitors. The anxiety, dread, and trauma that I experienced was horrifying. Why couldn't leadership just let me focus on the areas where I excelled? That would have made too much sense. Male show hosts were not required to sell fashion, but female show hosts had to sell everything. This infuriated me.

I felt oppressed, discriminated against, and devalued. Viewers loved me when I sold soft goods, but some wrote nasty letters to tell me how fat I was. I once told my overnight 3am to 6am viewers to turn the channel if I was so offensive. I got in major trouble for that comment. I got in major trouble for a lot of things, most prominently, for being a young black woman with a gift. I was hired for my personality and warmth, but I was forced to assimilate, conform, and fit into the culture. I could do nothing right...and I recognized this job was all wrong.

After nearly two years in the role of show host, I asked to be let out of my contract and embarked on a career as a freelance television host and actress. I landed a few juicy gigs. I auditioned and was hired as the New Jersey Lottery Host. This was such an honor because I watched the three-minute New Jersey Lottery Show for years with my grandfather, who bought $10 worth of lottery tickets on a daily basis. He would play and win often...never anything life-changing but he hit regularly. I imagined how amazed my grandfather would have been to see me host that show. His spirit was definitely with me...what a full-circle opportunity. The drive to Trenton, NJ to the NJN studio was about 40 minutes. I invested about 30 minutes in applying my makeup and getting dressed. The show was three minutes long. I announced the winning numbers and then jumped in my car to go back home. Because hosting the New Jersey Lottery Show was so quick and easy, I was able to do a variety of different things with my career. I held onto the Lottery gig for 14 years, until the show was cancelled after 40 years on the air.

Leveraging my tenacity and perseverance, I accomplished some pretty incredible things. I traveled the country conducting media tours on morning shows in just about every city you could name. I hosted a morning, home décor and craft show on HGTV and went to Nashville to record the episodes. I was hired by PBS as a Fundraising Host and raised millions of dollars for the network over the course of my 16 years with them. I worked for a full-figured magazine called MODE as a Fashion Retail Editor and visited Bloomingdale's, Neiman Marcus, Nordstrom, Macy's and other department stores to coordinate and commentate fashion shows. I toured along the East Coast in a theater production where I played one of the leads. I auditioned for and booked 50-plus commercials and corporate videos for major brands. I worked as a plus-size fit model in New York City for over five years. I even returned to the television shopping network as creator and spokesperson for my own clothing line.

Then all hell broke loose. On a hot summer day, as I was walking through Penn Station in NYC, running late for the train to return home after a fitting, I had what I came to understand was a panic attack. I had never experienced anything like this before in my entire life. Everything got vivid; I was spinning around in circles like an out-of-control top; my heart was racing 100 miles a minute; I felt like I was dying. I tried to make the train but missed it. I tried to call my mother but couldn't remember her number. I tried to understand what was happening to me but had no idea. What was wrong with me? What was happening to me? Was I dying? Was I going crazy?

Two weeks later, I was in a psych ward. The anxiety attack freaked me out so much that I eventually lost touch with reality and had a complete nervous breakdown. I was diagnosed as bipolar and given some drug that made me so groggy, I could barely function. I could not wrap my head around what was happening to me. I was beyond terrified and asked the doctors and nurses to explain why I was in this mess. The doctors threatened to keep me in the hospital longer, so I went into performance mode, stopped asking questions, and faked my way out of the psych ward by pretending to be fine. This would be the metaphor for my life. I would pretend to be fine when my world was falling apart.

The next several years would be filled with many twists and turns. I lost 85 pounds and gained it all back. I earned a Master of Arts in Higher Education Administration and discovered this new, innovative career called Life Coaching. The tone of the work resonated with me. I was finally able to feel connected with the pace and culture of my career as a coach. I started my own coaching practice but could not earn a living from just coaching. It was not sustainable, so I set a new goal to apply my Master's degree. I worked for respectable colleges and universities, but circumstances interrupted my ability to maintain longevity. The hierarchy was unbearable. I was stable for over two years in one role at a career institute but never felt content or fulfilled. I needed more. I craved connection with my work. I wanted to make a significant contribution. I wanted to make a difference. Despite the mental illness, I felt like I was capable of sinking my teeth into something meaningful.

Then everything changed. After being selected for a temporary "acting" role at a respectable university, I was replaced by a tall, white man with a life coaching background. He looked like a snake oil salesman, but he had captivated the administration and I was out of a job. I was absolutely crushed. I had a life coaching background. I had a Master's in higher education. The students were benefiting so much from my guidance. Why him and not me? I felt demoralized, marginalized, and mistreated. So I did what I always do...I went back to school again. I enrolled in a Life Coaching program that would positively change the entire course of my life. I got certified, re-started my coaching practice, and began to regain a sense of myself. I worked for a prestigious international automobile manufacturer as an Executive Coach and then with a small consulting firm as a consultant and coach. The work was fascinating, rich, and intentional. I was in love.

Coaching became my refuge. By 2016, I was able to utilize the skills I acquired to support people who were struggling. I was good at it and the work empowered me as I empowered others. Before I took this second stab at coaching, the bipolar diagnosis made me feel stigmatized. I rarely told anyone. I dated a man for over five years, and I didn't tell him. What I learned in coaching school was that vulnerability, sensitivity, compassion, and empathy were strengths. I realized that I took my own kindness for weakness and devalued my contribution because it involved soft skills.

During the time we were dating from 2009 to 2015, I went off my meds once because I was feeling so good. Foregoing medications is a bad habit that many with bipolar tend to have. I thought I didn't need the meds. I thought I could manage without them. I thought I would be okay. Unfortunately, I had another breakdown. Since I had a bit more expertise this time, I was able to coach myself through it and get the support I needed but my relationship was never the same. He felt betrayed. I felt entitled to keep my story. We broke up three years later. After I waited all that time for him to marry me, the man who didn't believe in marriage married someone else. I was devastated!

I honestly thought that our love would triumph over all the trauma and drama we endured. I was wrong. Instead, I struggled to find my identity without him. He was a sweet man...kind. This was the first real, loving relationship I had in my entire life. Growing up without a father, being undiagnosed as bipolar, and a survivor of sexual assault, I made many unwise choices when it came to men. Before him, I craved bad boys and longed for excitement, high energy, and passion. What I recognized was that although he and I loved each other very much, we were not ultimately meant to be together. We stayed together three years too long, but I was devoted to him and could not imagine life without him....90 pounds later, I was alone.

Eventually, I was the one who broke it off. How I mustered that courage, I will never know. I can only say what I always say when I feel pressed to leave a situation. My spirit was dying. I didn't just want to be married, I wanted to be married to him. I despised the idea of being his perpetual girlfriend. I knew he was the marrying kind but just didn't want to marry me. I never really thought about marriage and family until I met him. He was convinced that he didn't believe in marriage after his 22-year marriage failed. I knew better.

He was harboring resentment and frankly, judgment about my diagnosis. He was a high achiever, from an upper middle-class family, and very educated. His father had a doctorate and was the CEO of a hospital. He was raised with maids and reeked of that black elitism that made me want to literally vomit. I, on the other hand, came from a working-class family and was the first of my family to go to college. My grandmother was a maid. We had culture wars. "Return the damn shopping cart," I would say. "Why make people's jobs harder?" He didn't get it. People were there to serve him. He assumed that posture and refused to accept any thought that would make him feel marginalized or oppressed. Even though he was a black man, he had a wicked sense of entitlement. He was, though, in so many ways everything that I wanted to be…everything that I was striving to be. In spite of it all, I was proud of him…articulate, intelligent, successful. He took me to Maui when he won President's Club. I was the only girlfriend on the trip among wives. It was so uncomfortable.

I recognize that the culture wars were ultimately our downfall. He wanted a *Cosby Show* existence like his parents (although we know how that Cosby story turned out). And although I cleaned up nicely, I was no Claire Huxtable. I probably should have told him about my diagnosis but losing him was not an option for me. I waited too long. Besides, how do you break that news? "By the way, I take psychotropic drugs, have had three nervous breakdowns, been in a psych ward twice, and I'm diagnosed as bipolar." Yep, that is great dinner conversation. I was terrified that he would leave me, so I kept it from him and even hoped that it had gone away. This was the reason that I, out of sheer lack of judgment, stopped taking my medication.

This desire to pretend everything is okay is the one thing that has made me stumble more than once throughout my life. I make every effort to see the positive side, glass half full, rose-color glasses, Pollyanna perspective. Maybe that's why when I started bleeding uncontrollably and was told I needed a hysterectomy (after never having children), I pretended I was fine. I put my career first and never dedicated time or energy to starting a family. I rebelled against the idea. I didn't want to be tied down or slowed down. I admired women who made that choice, but it wasn't for me.

It was around that time that my 50th birthday was approaching. There was something monumental about that day, July 3, 2017. One day before, I received a text message from an old flame, asking if he could call me. He had bumped into a friend of mine in North Philadelphia and, like he had done periodically over the past couple decades, asked her about me. She gave him my number since she knew that I absolutely adored him. Tall, handsome, a smile that would light up the world, my ex-husband was the most sexy man I had ever known. His voice was deep and resonant. His hands were well-manicured but strong and masculine. He was a cross between Terrance Howard and LL Cool J and had a swagger that took my breath away. Until the day he walked out of my life, I was totally infatuated. I have never wanted something or someone more than I wanted him. Before I knew it, I was walking down the aisle, and I had assumed the role of wife to him and mother to his 11-year-old son.

His son, of whom he had custody, captured my heart. He was a tall, skinny kid with a heart of gold. Mild mannered...sweet natured. I had no children, and he had a complicated relationship with his mother. So I latched on...and so did he. We were two peas in a pod. I loved that young man. I was his mother for three years, until I wasn't.

It was clear to me that I wanted a family. Maybe I wanted the Cosby dream too. I knew on my honeymoon that I had made a mistake in judgment by marrying him. I spent the next two years trying to make our relationship work. I gave myself away and sacrificed everything. I lost my job, my home, almost quit my doctoral program, and even had to file for bankruptcy. In my time with him, I was not making smart decisions.

One day, he spoke to me again in that harsh, cruel, condescending tone, and it was the last straw. I remember calling a friend and saying, "I need to put leaving back on the table." I had taken it off the table as an option because I really wanted our marriage to work. Putting leaving back on the table meant I no longer believed in our vows, no longer chose to pretend everything was okay. On December 15, 2020, in the midst of a global pandemic, my divorce was final. After only two years of marriage, I had failed. I often say that I regret the marriage but not the divorce. I'm not sure what I expected, but it just didn't work. I can honestly say that my heart still skips a beat when I hear his name, but that divorce was the best gift I could have given myself.

About two weeks before the divorce was final, I successfully defended my dissertation. I now have an Ed.D. in Organizational Leadership... Dr. Renai Ellison...and, along with my education and experience as a Leadership Coach and Consultant, I am feeling similarly to that pivotal moment over 25 years ago, when I auditioned for that big television host job on the shopping channel. I'm having my Mary Tyler Moore moment and genuinely experiencing a shift in my attitude toward myself. I was just appointed as Interim Executive Director of a non-profit after a three-month consulting gig with the organization. My financial situation has corrected itself due to hard work and dedication. As I write this, I feel more blessed, more content, and more joyful than I have in ages.

Perseverance and tenacity have become my hallmark. I am humbled by the doors that God continues to open...and the ways God holds me accountable. I work daily on putting God first and remembering that it is through Him that all blessings flow. The idea of survival is not even an option. I refuse to just survive. I insist on thriving and finding creative ways to do it. By learning to be a progressive thinker, I can touch more lives and influence more people. I benefit daily from the love of a mother who is my rock and by cultivating friendships and relationships that are meaningful. When loneliness sets in (and it does), my prayer is to remain rooted in the Lord and to know that through God all things are possible. This next part of my life will be focused and dedicated to being the best creation I can be, and serving in a way that demonstrates respect for others and commitment to love, empathy, and deep compassion.

Charity Jones is the oldest born to a musical mother and father. She majored in music education at West Chester University, before working in the pre-school sector for several years. During that time, she was active in the Christian theater group, Actors for Christ and later, Chosen Vessels, as a writer, composer and actor.

After working several years in behavioral health for private agencies, Charity left that field to start and operate a pre-school music program called Handmade by Design. She later returned to behavioral health, working with adults while continuing to operate the music program. After successful certification as a music therapist, and completion of a Master of Arts music therapy program at Immaculata University, Charity began work as a Board-certified Music Therapist.

Charity currently works as a Hospice Music Therapist at Samaritan Life Enhancing Care in New Jersey. She is married with an adult son and daughter.

The Story of Allegra

CHARITY JONES

Getting pregnant again was the last thing on earth I wanted at the time. I was only 22. My husband and I, already the parents of a two-year-old boy, were not doing well at all in terms of our communication, interaction, or even just being in the same room together at times. Allegra's conception was, at best, a cruel joke by God when he was bored one day. Apart from our lack of love acts, I was in school, attempting for the second time to finish up my undergraduate degree. We were living on the third floor of a house used as my mother's day care, a floor with only three rooms, counting the bathroom. It was not a good time to get pregnant; a slap in the face for the birth control that we religiously used. I was so angry and so hurt at this development. I decided that God was no longer interested in the trials and tribulations of my life, and I needed to fix this myself. I am not a believer in abortion, but I was so overwhelmed with anger and hurt I had convinced myself that maneuvering an accident would not count as an abortion act, and it was worth a possible injury to myself in the process. I planned to throw myself down a flight of stairs. As I mustered up the courage to fling myself, my precious Savior had his angels ready. I could not move. I would lift my foot to go forward, but I was pushed back. You cannot tell me that miracles do not happen. God physically kept me from doing a horrible act. After trying three times, I sat on the top step and cried. How could I possibly bring this child into a relationship where love felt so lost? Where would we keep her? Where would the money come from?

Have you ever felt the presence of God when you are in the depths of despair? There have been times in life when I've been alone, yet felt a holy presence holding me up. And that is what I felt that day, the presence of the Lord. And as I got up from the step and went to tend to my chores, I knew that the Lord had a plan. And I had to trust in His plan.

Part of that plan apparently was not to finish school at that time. About three months into the pregnancy, I started spotting. A visit to the doctor did little to reveal the mystery. I was told that the daily travel to school would be too stressful. Additionally, I was having pains in my side and headaches for which no explanation could be found. As I tended to my two-year-old, I thought about what life would be like having two babies under the age of three. The more I tried to imagine it, the more I had a strong feeling that I would not see this baby growing inside me grow to adulthood. I kept that secret in my heart, not daring to share it with anyone, lest it become true.

I am the type of person who does not do well sitting at home, so I needed to find an activity that would keep me occupied yet keep my baby safe. My aunt was a teacher, so I became a volunteer in her class three times a week. This way, family was looking out for me, and I got out of the house and out of the worries that constantly clogged my mind. Nevertheless, a lingering sadness stayed with me, always. I wanted to find peace in all that was happening, but I could not find it anywhere. We still had no means to move, we still were not on the best of terms, and the pains persisted. In an attempt to locate the source of the pain, my doctor instituted a series of tests, the results of which seemed to indicate that my baby had a deformity. I was told that there was a possibility that my child had Spina Bifida. You can imagine how overwhelmed I felt. How on earth would I take care of a special needs child, when I felt I could barely take care of the rambunctious boy I already had? Was this punishment for my anger in the earlier months?

As I was processing all of my thoughts, I received a call from another hospital. The receptionist on the line informed me that they were given my name as someone who was looking to abort a deformed baby. She sounded almost gleeful as she asked for a date and time when she could schedule me to get rid of my "inconvenience." How the hand of God moved on me in that instant. I told that receptionist that I had no intention on getting rid of any child that I carried. She reminded me, almost angrily, that I was told that my baby was deformed, which would mean a life of heartache. I told her then so be it. It was right then that I knew God was going to take care of it all. In that moment, I fell in love with that child in my womb, and somehow knew that it was a girl who would be my joy. After this event, my doctor scheduled me for an ultrasound, one that would be very thorough to examine all sides of my uterus for verification of what was diagnosed. A few days after that procedure that took well over an hour, I received the news. My baby was fine. There was no evidence of Spina Bifida.

As the pregnancy continued, I started thinking of creative ways to find room for her in our tiny space. As a musician, I knew very well the importance of music in early childhood. I sang to my baby belly daily. I spoke to her, telling her how much she was loved and that she had a father and a brother who could not wait to see her. I would smile when I felt her move in response to my voice. It would be all right. Somehow, it would be all right.

Christmas was on a Sunday that year. There were wonderful times with family and presents. When I started feeling unwell, I figured it was all the excitement. The stuffy head and scratchy throat was a simple cold. When the fever developed, I took medicine after consulting with the doctor. I forced myself to play with my little boy and his new toys. I felt my baby girl moving around inside, even though it felt like she was curling into a tight ball, like every 30 minutes. I thought that maybe it was too much with the cold medicine and jumping around with the boy, so after I put him to bed, I took a bath to calm down and relax. My husband was working overnight at the time, and it was New Year's Eve. After the bath, I spoke with friends and family members on the phone, sharing new year wishes. One of my friends said that it sounded like I was having a hard time breathing. I was becoming breathless in the middle of sentences. I explained to her that I had cramping, but it was probably just Braxton-Hicks. I was fine. I really tried to make myself believe that.

Around midnight, I started having an urgent need to go to the bathroom. There was a thought that maybe I should call my doctor. Fear convinced me that it would be nonsense to bother my doctor on a holiday. I could always call her the day after New Year's Day. Can you imagine? I tried to get some sleep, but literally every five to ten minutes from midnight to around 2 am, I was getting up to go to the bathroom. When my mucus plug came out, I called the doctor in a panic. Then I called my parents, who came right away. I did not want to believe that I was so strongly in labor. It was so surreal. As they managed to get me into the car, a wave of excruciating pain hit me, and I bit down on a towel, screaming through the whole ride to the hospital. I remember seeing a grim look on my father's face as he raced through the empty streets in the middle of the night. When we arrived at the hospital, the doctor was standing at the emergency room entrance ready to meet us. My water gushed out and down my legs as I stepped out of the car. As they rushed me into the elevator to the labor and delivery floor, I kept asking, "What is happening to me? What is happening?"

It turns out that I was 10 centimeters dilated. I was 100 percent effaced. The doctor couldn't understand how I didn't give birth in the car. I was set up for an emergency C-section, as there was concern that the trauma of the birth canal would be fatal for the baby. I was put to sleep, and at 3:29 am on January 1, my Allegra Danielle was born. Allegra means "Joyful." Her name and her presence expressed the hope that my husband and I both shared that somehow her presence would bring joy back into our lives. She weighed 1 pound, 5 ounces, and was born at 25 weeks' gestation. They woke me up so that I could see this little miracle. I cradled her tiny head in my hand; it was so small and round. Then she was rushed to a neo-natal center for care in another hospital about a mile away.

Unfortunately, I had acquired an infection, which kept me in the hospital for several days with a fever. I could not go see my baby. My husband was so instrumental in making sure I knew how our little one was doing. He went to see her in the unit every day, twice a day, before and after work. He took pictures of her, then he would come to see me and show me how she looked. She had a head full of hair, jet black and straight. We spoke to each other. We shared our fears about the future, and our joy at having a daughter. I was so grateful to my husband for taking those pictures. Between running from one hospital to another and going to work, he hardly had any time for himself. As the hours passed during my hospital stay, I marveled at the fact that I was a mother to a son and daughter. I knew how serious my Allegra's situation was, and I was so worried. Why did this happen? Was it my fault? Was God punishing me for being angry at the beginning of the pregnancy? My mother reminded me of Romans 8:28, "And we know that all things work together for good, to those that love God, to those that are called according to His purpose." But what could possibly be the purpose in having this little girl so early like this?

My husband and I had a meeting with Allegra's doctors. They were careful to tell us that she had a long road ahead. Most of her organs were fairly well developed if she was still in the womb; outside the womb was a different matter altogether. They predicted that she would most likely have to stay in the hospital till at least April. Four months. So many questions again in my mind. *How will I do this? How can we afford for me not to work?* I began to have headaches from the fear and the worry, which did not help my infection to heal at all. As I shared my concerns with friends who would call and come to check on me, all were encouraging. But no one had experienced what I was experiencing, and they could not give me the concrete answers I was looking for. Then one day, I was speaking to a minister friend, sharing my frustration about everything, and the fact that I was not getting any answers. He simply told me, "Maybe it's not meant for you to get all the answers."

"Well, how can I help my baby?" I said. "How can I make an informed decision about what is best for everything and everyone?"

He gently said to me, "Just seek after God. Rest in Him. Praise Him for all that He is doing right now." He gave me Psalm chapter 42 and instructed me to read it every day. There was something so very comforting about reading, "Why art thou cast down, o my soul? And why art thou disquieted within me? Hope thou in God; for I shall yet praise Him, the help of my countenance and my God." This chapter was what kept my sanity during those days in the hospital when I could not get to my baby. It kept me calm when speaking to the doctors by phone every day regarding her progress. It was what I had read earlier on the sixth day after giving birth when I was called by a doctor whose voice I did not recognize, who told me that my daughter had taken a turn for the worse. Her vital signs were dropping, and she was not expected to make it through the night. I remember hearing this strange voice on the phone while sitting in my hospital room and thinking, *Someone is playing a horrible joke on me! Who would call me and say such a thing?*

As I questioned this man, there was a growing realization that he was speaking the truth. There were too many details shared. As he continued to speak on all that they were trying to do to keep my baby alive, I began to scream. It started as a small sound in the back of my throat until it filled the room. It took a while for me to realize the sound was coming from me. Nurses ran into the room. One grabbed the phone from me and began to interrogate who was on the other end. The other just held me, rocking me as I cried. I had to get out of there. I had to go to my baby, the baby I had never got to hold in my arms. Those nurses were wonderful. They gave me street clothes to wear, as my husband had taken home what I wore to the hospital and had not gotten a chance to bring any clothes back. The one nurse contacted the last person who I had spoken to on the phone, and that friend agreed to come pick me up from the hospital and take me to see Allegra. I still had a fever, and was shaky with chills, but nothing was going to keep me from seeing this child at the end of her life. My friend got me into the car and prayed as we sped down the road to the other hospital. I was frantic. When we arrived at the emergency room door of the other hospital, I stamped my feet in response to questions by the security guard and demanded to be allowed in. Fortunately, my friend was able to explain my behavior. "Jesus," I kept crying in the elevator, "Jesus, I need you now!"

When I arrived to the NICU, the nurses were waiting for me, along with so many members of my family. My friend had managed to call my mother who got the word out. My husband had even gotten there, having left work early. They were all there with hugs and tears. The doctor who spoke with me on the phone met with us in the waiting room, again explaining the sad truth. Allegra's trachea was just not developed enough to sustain her. And her other organs were failing as well. I asked if she were to live through the night, would she have a chance for recovery. The doctor looked so mournful as he shook his head and stated that she would be a vegetable.

Now right there, most people who believe in the healing power of God would at once initiate a cloud-shaking prayer of healing. But God's ways are not our ways. I understood right then what it means to have the peace that passes all understanding. It was like a stillness of acceptance and tranquility washed over me. I asked if I could please hold my Allegra. The nurses led me to her little cubicle and began to gently remove all her tubes. I marveled at what I saw: a beautiful child who looked exactly like her father. She was about the length of a sheet of paper. They wrapped her in a blanket and gave her to me. I walked to the rocking chair and sat down. I just could not take my eyes off this precious gift whose life was being used for God's glory. I began to sing to her, watching and feeling her taking her last little breath. And there was peace. After my pastor prayed over Allegra and me, the nurses took her and gently put her back in her bed. I began to go around the room, thanking and hugging everyone there, telling them it was all right. She was with Jesus.

The peace inside me remained, sharing space with the sadness. I tried to find anger; I tried to find hurt. But it just wasn't there. My husband and I held each other up. We began to talk to each other. We shared a singular life-changing experience. We had lost a child.

I expressed to him how proud of him I was for his part and how grateful for his diligence in looking after us every day in two separate hospitals, while working full time. He shared his love for me and all that I had endured in the pregnancy, resolving to be steadfast at my side. Gradually our conversations turned to the nature of our marriage, and we used the common ground of grief to begin building the steps of trust.

And so life continues. There were many more days of disagreement, and many more days of joy. We have a daughter in heaven. As I resigned myself to that fact, the Lord blessed us with another daughter two years later. We named her Aliyah Gabrielle, her name meaning "perfect angel of God." The things I was personally trying to accomplish back then have been accomplished and then some, by the united mission of my husband and me working together. Allegra's life was a gift, given and shared by a loving Heavenly Father who knows what to do for us all individually in the most intimate and unique way—a gift that will never be forgotten. For the whole experience, I am forever grateful.

Gina H. Curry is a change agent and visionary for advocacy and activism for equity. She has been an educator with over 20 years of experience working with youth and families through K-12, the collegiate level and in practice. She studied and earned both her bachelor's and master's degrees in Criminal Justice with a concentration on Sociology from St. Joseph's University. Along with her talents in the classroom and professional environments to educate, mentor, and lead, Gina has vast experiences in the behavioral health field as a clinical supervisor, behavioral specialist and therapeutic consultant to children and families. Her passionate desire to educate, engage and develop strong communities has led her in the direction of entrepreneurship and civic engagement.

Gina and her husband, Rap set their vision forward and formed Curry Real Estate Group, LLC over eight years ago with the mission of empowering the restructuring of community assets and increasing knowledge among young adults and the importance of property ownership and wealth building. She also serves as an owner of her own consulting business, Coach Your Vision, LLC, where she continually drives enthusiasm in training, curriculum writing and education consulting services as a DEI and Social Justice consultant.

Gina was elected in 2017 and again in 2019, as a School Board Director in Upper Darby, PA after an engaged campaign built on equity and representation for the underfunded school district where she resides. Her strong understanding of her community needs and fairness in education and real estate continues to help her advocate and fight for the best education for all children.

Out of District: Navigating Homelessness and Housing Insecurities

GINA H. CURRY

I had everything that I needed but I had no idea what that meant… God had a plan for my life. God could see ME and absolutely knew where I would land. He was focused on covering me in areas that I could not possibly imagine would lead me to who I am today and His purpose for me and only me. "'For I know the plans I have for you,' declares the LORD, 'plans to prosper you and not to harm you, plans to give you hope and a future'" (Jeremiah 29:11).

My very first vivid and unforgettable memory of what I was missing in my young life was more than apparent to my seven-year-old self. As a matter of fact, it was this event that would help me to know that I was being sheltered from the very heartache that would follow me through my life and ultimately help me understand the burning fire in my heart to create safe spaces, fight for the voiceless, the marginalized…to seek out the powerful potential that could undoubtedly change the world. "Perhaps this is the moment for which you have been created" (Esther 4:14). It was a regular day. I was in the second grade at Chadwick Elementary School. I was 7 years old. I was well fed, well-dressed, my hair was brushed in place with colorful barrettes on the ends of each twisted braid…four out of four and I was ready for my day.

What I did not know about was the agonizing, intense struggle my parents were faced with as they dropped me and my siblings off to start our day. The unforgiving truth was that we were hours away from EVICTION…HOUSING   DISPARITY…HOMELESSNESS. While I was at school, there was a whirlwind of navigation, a stress-filled frenzy and the 'unknown' loomed with high anticipation. My mother and father were unable to save the safe place that we had known, the security of a warm bed, the regularity of knowing where we were going and the budding friendships from the neighborhood kids who were clueless regarding the struggle because I was unaware myself. It was not the first time we were being pushed to move because of financial deficiency but it was the first time that I got a large dose of reality because that morning would be the last time that I would see my apartment, my room that I shared with my younger sister, access to our community pool on those hot summer days, walks to our mom-and-pop local spot to fill up on sugar and sweets and the overall security that my neighborhood represented…even if it was temporary. I do not remember much about my school day, but I will never forget the end of it. Dismissal came; kids scattered to get to their next destination. Friends waving goodbye, students leaving the building to meet their parents, big brothers and sisters and caregivers, jumping on busses, and hopping in cars that were there waiting in anticipation for their delivery home.

My experience was quite different that day. I remember my mother telling me to wait for her after school and she would be there to pick me up. My sister had a half day because she was in kindergarten and my brother…well, I am not exactly clear but knowing him, he was probably allowed to go hang out with friends before baseball practice began. So I waited and waited and waited and waited. Everyone cleared out for dismissal, student safeties left their posts, crossing guards moved toward their cars, teachers cleared out of the parking lot, and the sound of silence was overwhelming...I knew I was alone. This was a first. I was questioning in my little mind...did my family really forget to pick me up from school? Well, on this day they did. They forgot seven-year-old Gina. They forgot me. What I did not know or even begin to understand is WHY, what was going on at that very moment. There were no cell phones to check in or give a quick reminder, and we did not live close, so it was not like I could just take a chance and walk home, and I remembered clearly the instructions my mother gave me: to wait.

After being obedient to what I was told but knowing that some-thing had changed, I walked back up to the school building doors and walked back inside. I moved toward the main office, feeling nervous, teary-eyed and confused as to why no one came for me. I was approached by a gentle giant and had no clue how this would change my life. My assistant principal asked me why I was still there. Mr. Walker was unforgettable. His tall, unassuming stature placed a shadow of familiarity over me. He stood about 6'3" or 6'4" tall and his demeanor was gentle yet commanding. I knew I had found a safe space in all the uncertainty. He was there to help, and I felt it when I needed it the most. Mr. Walker sprang into action as his workday was ending, but that did not seem to matter. He went searching for my emergency contact card, securely filed in the office, and started making calls with no success.

What we did not know was that my mother missed her scheduled pick-up time because she was securing a moving van, gathering our belongings, and making critical decisions to save our family dignity. Making sure that our life, as we knew it, was not just moved out carelessly on the curb, as we had seen it happen many times before to those families in that same neighborhood who were forced out before us. As the late hour approached and we still had no answers, no contact and no reasonable explanation, Mr. Walker made the decision to locate my home address listed on the card, put me in the back seat of his car and take me home. Thinking back on how policies and procedures have changed so drastically on child safety and welfare, this option would never have been available today. The authorities would have been notified and the already tragic circumstances that were swirling in my family life would have been exacerbated without even understanding the painful, uncontrollable events that would alter what I had known to be my security only 12 hours earlier.

I can remember feeling better with his decision, knowing that in a matter of minutes I would see my mother and knowing that everything was going to be okay. I remember feeling safe and secure with Mr. Walker and that his ultimate care for me was calming and reassuring. I remember feeling a sense of stability on that car ride, not knowing that our cover would be blown that day, once Mr. Walker realized that my family was living 'out of district.' The ride that should have taken less than 10-15 minutes in any one direction due to school lines, boundaries, and limits, took over 25 -30 minutes in the rush hour delays. "Those moments when you just can't put your prayers into words, God hears your heart" (Unknown). The question swirling around in my young mind wouldn't let me sit with how Mr. Walker got our 'real' address. How did he know to take me to our hidden residence? The residence that could not have possibly been listed on the emergency contact card. The place where we lived…out of district!

When we arrived at the opening of the driveway of our apartment complex, I was anxious with anticipation to see my mother, my father or anyone in my family at that could grab me, hug me, and hold me tight. Familiarity and comfort were what I so desperately longed for after an afternoon of insecure uncertainty. We pulled up to the front of my building, where there were several long, wide steps and about five to six steps to climb before reaching the glass doorway with the metal bar to open the door. We lived on the second floor. As we pulled up no one was waiting with anticipation to greet me and then suddenly the door opened, and it was our neighbor from the next building over. She came out to meet me, thanked Mr. Walker for bringing me home safely and grabbed my hand to help me out of the car. She shut the big heavy door and we waved as Mr. Walker made his way back out of our complex, most likely with many uncomfortable thoughts of concern, apprehension, and rigid enforcement.

That day my family was evicted from that secret address. We had nowhere to move and we had officially entered the status of homelessness. Along with the eviction, my parents had to physically separate to accommodate adequate temporary housing until they were able to land permanency and most importantly, the priority was finding housing within the district. Fortunately, we did not have to sleep on the streets, in a shelter or in our car that night. We were taken to my aunt's apartment complex around the corner from my elementary school for a secure place to lay our heads while my mother sorted it all out. She welcomed us with open arms. I remember having to be extremely quiet in my aunt's small apartment for what seemed like weeks because her apartment complex did not allow children. It was not at all equipped for two additional adults and three children. We also stayed with another aunt and my grandmother in West Baltimore for a stint, where we camped out on the living room floor with sleeping bags and blankets and pretended we were on an extended camping trip in the city. My great-grandfather would faithfully pick us up before the sun came up each morning to take us back to the 'in district' boundaries for school.

We were homeless for several weeks, maybe even a few months, before we moved into our next apartment within walking distance of the school. The trauma of suddenly being left at school that day, being forced to leave the stability of the home I knew and the absence of my father because we just did not have enough space left a lasting memory that has stayed in my heart throughout my life. It was just the beginning of more transition. It was the beginning of the way I viewed the instability of where I lived and the frequency of moving when financial insecurities prevailed. The one clear fact that I was sure of at the time was that my mother and father were attempting to provide the absolute best for me and my siblings. Our education always mattered. My mother and father had not made a mistake by revealing our 'out of district' address that day, yet Mr. Walker knew exactly where to drop me off. I never asked and we never discussed it again.

We started our elementary school experience at Chadwick Elementary because my parents made the decision to leave Baltimore City and move to Baltimore County. They initially moved into an apartment complex behind the school and then transitioned to a three-bed-room townhouse in Chadwick Manor. It was a modest townhouse community located in Woodlawn, Maryland. This was considered the suburbs of Baltimore and the school district was the Baltimore County Public School System. My parents were proud and comfort-able with their decision to start our education in this blue-collar, working-class community with an inkling of diversity that had just begun to surface. My mother was an educator by trade. She was a teacher who specialized in English on the primary and middle school levels and a guidance counselor. My father was a construction worker who specialized in bricklaying. Their priority was keeping us focused, involved, and moving toward preparation for higher education. We lived comfortably, at least from my childhood perspective, for almost the next six years, until homelessness struck yet again, ripping my family apart for good. Financial and housing insecurities followed us throughout my childhood, only to return through eviction in the March of my senior year in high school. That was the breaking point for my family.

"Be still and know the I am God" (Psalm 46:10). My family was devastated by financial instability, housing insecurities, separation, and divorce over the span of my childhood and my young adult life. The trauma of these experiences was meant to break me, end my journey to find my purpose and drown out any hope for healing, peace, and housing stability. The circumstances moved my father into separating from us both physically and emotionally. The absence of his presence was deeply felt. My mother was our rock. I have strong memories of her making quick decisions, like a BOSS, that helped us to move into the next best space. We saw her move in this leadership with our education, our social development and through the navigation of being our spiritual mentor. She taught us how to be still and trust God. My mother continued to stay committed to our family and pushed us to greatness through her perseverance and unwavering faith. She had to trust and depend on God's grace and mercy to pull us through, and He did just that. With God's guidance and faithfulness, my mother kept us on track for the journey that molded each of us into who we are today. She continued to rent and rebuild and became a homeowner in 1998, where she still resides 23 years later. I am forever grateful!

Being still and trusting God for His next steps in my life began to be my focus. I was able to finish high school in June of 1990, just three months shy of our last housing transition/eviction from our home to stay with my uncle 25 miles south of our last house. It also put me farther away from my high school on the east side of Baltimore City. While my classmates were buzzing around preparing for senior activities, finishing up college applications and choosing their dresses for prom, I was trying to navigate packing boxes and moving our belongings into storage until further notice. It was all a struggle. My circumstances presented many stressors that would present repeatedly as I moved on to attend college in Philadelphia that fall. "But those who wait upon the Lord shall renew their strength; they shall mount up with wings like eagles; they shall run and not be weary; and they shall walk and not faint." Isaiah 40:31, KJV

Moving into the next stage for me was monumental—a new space that I considered mine and understood once again that this stage would be temporary but purposeful. I had a chance to change my trajectory through higher education. I had hopes to end my feelings of fear, instability, and paralysis around standing up to the internal stigma that had plagued me since second grade—thoughts that attached to my thinking of inadequacies, not being enough or even capable of changing the narrative that I have lived with my whole life. I worked tirelessly through college, like so many, to find ways to finance my education through the painstaking double shifts, working multiple jobs and taking student loans to support my vision and dreams to become more. I graduated with my Bachelor's degree and followed that up with the completion of my graduate degree two years later. I was young, educated, and ready to make my mark on the world. But...it did not quite work out that way.

Full of hopes and dreams, I entered the workforce with a plan and mission to wait on God for His next best plan for me, all the while still holding too much space for my past trauma that continued to stand in the way of my true purpose and peace. I spent many years searching for the happiness that would make things right, but I found out that the pursuit of happiness was really about the joy I experienced when I began to advocate for others. I started with my own children. When I was blessed to start my family, I transitioned into a place of activism, advocacy and community engagement around their wellbeing and the focus on their education from their early childhood years onward. What became crystal clear was the idea that I had to be present to ensure the best for my children and all children involved. "For if you remain silent at this time, relief and deliverance for the Jews will arise from another place, but you and your father's family will perish. And who knows but that you have come to your royal position for such a time as this." Esther 4:14, NIV

Having everything I needed still was not resonating. Years of doubt, conflict, and unrest within myself persisted and even as I began to grow in my faith, trust, and relationship with the Lord, I still was not living my life in His full abundance. At this point, my adult life as was in full swing, as a wife, a mother, and a homeowner. My father never got to see my adult accomplishments because he died in 1999. God continued to show me His plans and was positioning me over the years. The early 2000s were impactful. I had two children of my own and began to get involved with the home and school association at their preschool, which led to more involvement when they got to elementary school. Parent and community involvement became my priority. In 2016, I was encouraged to become involved at a higher level. I was asked to run for the school board in my district. I am not a politician by any means, but I am a fighter for equity, justice, and fairness. My grassroots efforts prepared me for the challenge. I won that challenge. I ran in 2017 for a two-year seat and won. I ran again in 2019 for a four-year seat and won with the highest number of votes in my district across every seat! I have also been sought after to run for various state level positions.

I have graduated from passion to purpose. I am now serving the children, families, and my community as the first female Black

Vice-President of the Upper Darby School District. I am a warrior in the fight for the children in my district and throughout Pennsylvania. While trauma can be a place that will cause us to want to fail, quit or even give up, I now know my trauma has been used to show up for those who cannot show up at all. All those years of depression and oppression have turned into progression. God positioned me for a time such as this for me to speak up, step up and be an influencer for truth, justice and His kingdom. These positions of power and influence are no different than the position of seven-year-old Gina. God has used my path to lift up the journey of others, and the best part is I always had everything I needed, even when I was out of district.

Monique Johnson is a native New Yorker from St. Albans, Queens. Currently, she resides in Windsor Mill, Maryland. A graduate of The University of Maryland: Eastern Shore, she obtained a Bachelor of Science in Special Education. Ms. Johnson furthered her studies and attended Towson University, in which she obtained a Master of Education in Early Childhood.

Ms. Johnson, a veteran Special Education Teacher with Baltimore City Public Schools, has provided over 27 years of dedicated service to children and their families. Currently, Ms. Johnson provides specialized instruction to children with special needs, in which many of them have Autism. She lends behavioral and academic support to families of special needs children.

Education is not Ms. Johnson's only passion and accomplishment. Entrepreneurship is prevalent, alongside her career in education. Taking inspiration from her maternal grandmother, who suffered from Arthritis and Dementia. Ms. Johnson enrolled and graduated from the Baltimore School of Massage. She is a Licensed Massage Therapist in the state of Maryland, and the proud owner of Lavender Dreams Mobile Spa.

Live Life Right Now!

Fatherless Daughter

MONIQUE JOHNSON

It amazes me how the absence of a father can impact your adult life. My parents divorced when I was such a youngster. The dynamics of divorce shaped my life as a woman. It left an imbalance and disrupted the family fabric that I once had. Mom and Dad were no longer; it became just Mom. I was far too young to fully understand that this imbalance would create many life lessons as I navigated and pushed through obstacles and challenges.

Fathers are to protect, love, provide, affirm, validate, and help build self-confidence and self-esteem. They are to demonstrate the blueprint of how a woman should be treated by a man. Unfortunately, I did not have that blueprint. Growing up, my father was absent. I was abandoned.

As I take a closer look at my family dynamics, I realize there are many fatherless daughters. Some became fatherless through divorce, death, broken relationships, or a father who was emotionally unavailable. There are too many women raising their children alone or with limited support. Often, some of these women rely on the support of other family members to help raise their children.

During my childhood, I had many fond memories despite not having my father around. As a child, I was creative, nurturing, kind, loving, inquisitive, observant, a visionary, and chatty. Throughout school, I participated in a multitude of extracurricular activities, such as camp, dance, school choir, track and field, and cheerleading.

Growing up, I did not think about my father. He was, as the saying goes, "out of sight, out of mind." My father was never "bad-mouthed" and was not banned from seeing his children. After many years, my father wanted a reunion with his children. I believe that I was either late elementary school age or the beginning of middle school. It was a Meet-and-Greet. My father and I were complete strangers. The encounter felt strange and awkward. As a young child, I had no clue what to do, but just smile and be friendly. Respect was given because he was my father. After that encounter with my father, I never saw him again until my adult years.

As I reflect on my childhood, there were not too many strong, positive males in my presence. As a child, I was always observant. I observed how some of the boys were treated in the family. It appeared that they received more time and attention. Although I was a young girl, I longed to participate in many of their activities, such as going fishing, or reading Bible scriptures together. In my mind, I wanted to bond and have that "father" connection. There were other males in my presence, but it did not fill that void left by my father.

Throughout my childhood, I soon realized the differences between the genders. Some men in my family were groomed from an early age in how to treat women and girls. Often, I would see injustices play out right before my eyes. When these injustices took place, I would bravely speak up against them. I was extremely inquisitive and would always question situations. Due to my age, I would always be told to stay in a "child's place" and to stay out of "grown folks'" business. My voice was silenced. My opinion or feelings did not matter.

As a youngster, I always stood out from the crowd. I never was a follower and walked to the beat of a different drum. Socially, I made friends and enjoyed their company. However, I would be content by myself, in my own peace. Peace was important in my life. I had fit the profile of being an introvert-extrovert. However, there was not always peace.

Throughout the years, I have observed unhealthy interactions and situations amongst adults. Familiar men, younger or older, in my presence, did not always treat women well. It was traumatic, disrespectful, and disappointing. I looked up to these men. I have observed some women being treated poorly. These women were treated second-best, belittled, bullied, ignored, threatened, abused (emotionally, verbally, physically), disrespected, controlled, manipulated, and silenced.

There were pockets of these interactions and situations throughout my life. Toxic behaviors and unhealthy relationships were normalized. Unconsciously, I adopted a policy of tolerating many behaviors from men and in some instances, friendships. I did not observe many positive, healthy relationships or how to learn healthy coping mechanisms.

It is my belief that if my father had been present and demonstrated healthy behaviors himself, then my life would have been shaped differently. My father experienced childhood trauma and he did not heal from it. It is sad and so unfortunate because he missed great moments with his children. I can count on one hand the number of encounters I had with my father. He continues to abandon and demonstrate a "victim mentality." Initially, it used to bother me, not having a relationship with my father. However, as time moved on, I have forgiven him and healed from my own childhood trauma.

As an impressionable young girl, I struggled with low confidence, low self-esteem, feeling invisible, and not having a voice. I did not feel pretty, smart, or good enough, when I would compare myself to other girls. In school, I made friends but would often compare myself to the confident ones. Many of them had their fathers or older brothers in their life.

As a young adult, I continued to struggle with low self-esteem, low confidence, no self-respect, feeling invisible, voiceless, and unworthiness. Often, I looked to receive validation or approval from others. I cared about what people thought about me, their impressions of me.

During college, I was drawn to "bad boys" or guys with an "edge" because of my experiences growing up. The guys I dated were often older than me. They were charming, charismatic, and aesthetically pleasing. It was thrilling and exciting initially, until unwanted behaviors began to surface. There was always a darker side. I would always go with the flow and tolerate bad behavior. Often, I would allow others to take me for granted, including so-called friendships. I was naïve and blindsided by many. I have encountered many situations that were unhealthy. God protected and delivered me from people, places, and situations that were meant for my harm.

Growing up, I was always a nurturer. I have nurtured people and animals. I was driven by taking care of someone or something. In many cases, this was my kryptonite because I wanted to always "fix" problems or people please. Being "Ms. Fix-It" was not always best because I did not know boundaries. In relationships (romantic, family, and friendships), I would always be the "nice one" and tolerate toxic behaviors and put others' needs before mine. Voice suppression was a common denominator. I would not speak up many times and just go with the flow. I would make excuses for other's behaviors.

Throughout college and my early professional days, I had to navigate through life the best way that I knew how. I did not always make the best decisions. Some decisions were not proud moments. At 17 years of age, I left for college. I turned 18 in early August. I had embarked on a life-changing journey.

Moving out of state for college was the best life-changer for GROWTH. It shaped my mindset and outlook on life. New experiences were presented or created. College life was great for the most part. There were so many lessons learned about relationships. I have met some interesting people along the way. Some of those people were intriguing and I was drawn into their world, a world that was fast-paced and unforgiving at times. I was so naïve and gullible back then. There were toxic situations that occurred. I have observed situations that were negative. Jealousy and envy were prevalent, and I felt the wrath for not seeing red flags, when presented. I did not know about having boundaries. I had no protocol to follow when dealing with certain relationships and friendships. Simply, I learned as I went along. However, God still had a great plan for my life, and I was divinely protected.

As I entered the professional workforce after college, I endured unique challenges. Boundaries were not a part of my life. I needed guidance. I was a young woman making it on her own. I needed my father. I needed my father to help me through life's twists and turns. I needed a man's perspective when it came to dating. As stated, I was a people pleaser and "Ms. Fix-It" when it came to relationships, family, and friendships. This behavior transitioned into the workplace. I wanted to be the "nice" one who went with the flow and did not make waves. My personal life and professional life mirrored each other. I sought validation and acceptance. Due to being abandoned at such an early age by my father, I was often disappointed when others did not value me. Abandonment weaved its way in. I would go out of my way to satisfy the needs of others, while depleting my own needs. Time, mental health, wellness, money and energy were sacrificed.

I had three encounters as an adult with my father. During our encounters, he would offer an apology and make promises of remaining in touch. Abandonment crept in again, along with empty promises and major disappointment. Upon reflection, there is a strong correlation between my father's behaviors/actions and the impact that they had in my life. I wanted my father's love and attention, his adoration, his validation, his protection, and his presence. Each day was a search, and I poured my entire being into everything and anything that came my way. And by doing this, I became depleted, exhausted, and lost my self-respect. I had lost myself, my voice, my will, my worth, my wellbeing. I OVER-GAVE to family, relationships, friendships, and work, while others TOOK. There were no healthy boundaries established.

Empathy is one of the behaviors that I demonstrate toward others. When others hurt, I feel their pain intensely. I do not like to see others in pain, and I always want to help them. However, based on experiences and situations, I have learned to take a step back and allow a higher power to intervene. God had to intervene because I developed behaviors with codependency. I had put myself in the role of caregiver. Being in this role allowed me to feel needed and wanted. My intentions to help others in any way that I could came at a cost. Family, work, friendships, and relationships took over my life. I wanted to save everyone except myself. My life was not important because I wanted to take care of others and their baggage. As time progressed, God opened my eyes to what was important: ME. I had lost ME. ME had sacrificed her energy, time, well-being, money, goals, and personal development.

During my thirties, I began to think about having children. I have always longed for that perfect scenario. I wanted a healthy marriage to raise children in. Children should be brought into this world with two healthy parents. Unfortunately, there is not always a perfect scenario. In fact, nothing is perfect. Healthy individuals have their ups and downs as well, but they create a loving, safe, respectful, and peaceful environment, an environment which displays a natural affection and love for women and children. The Fruits of the Spirit should be prevalent. 1 Corinthians 13:4-8, NIV reads, "We are nothing without love: Love is patient, love is kind. It does not envy, it does not boast, it is not proud. It does not dishonor others, it is not self-seeking, it is not easily angered, it keeps no record of wrongs. Love does not delight in evil but rejoices with the truth. It always trusts, always hopes, always perseveres. Love never fails."

Children, I believe, are blessings from God. They are so precious and pure. I have often wondered throughout the years, as to why I never had children. God has placed a patient, kind, loving, and nurturing spirit inside me. There was a time when I would check out my biological clock and stress over having children. Thankfully, God had other plans for my life. Although I did not physically birth children, God blessed me with an occupation that filled that void completely. I used to get upset and feel bad that I did not have children. I have come to the realization that having children did not define me. It did not validate me as a woman. Having children was an option and it's unselfish to not have them.

In my younger years, honestly, as I reflect on my relationships, I am blessed to not have had children. Those relationships would have resulted in single motherhood. Some of those relationships were toxic and abusive. I WAS CHOOSING MEN LIKE MY FATHER. Digging deep, I did not want that scenario for my children. I have seen too much dysfunction in my life and wanted better. CHILDREN ARE IMPACTED BY ADULT CHOICES. They do not ask to be born into this world to suffer abuse and neglect. Every child should have two healthy parents to help groom and mold them into healthy adults. Proverbs 22:6 KJV reads, "Train up a child in the way he should go. And when he is old, he will not depart from it. Teach children how they should live, and they will remember it all their life." When healthy parents are not present, the toxic cycle continues to repeat and become a stronghold on that child's life. These strongholds create strife and a difficult, painful life, until something gives. Hopefully, wanting more and striving for more would be the motivation to create a better life. These cycles of abuse and neglect need to come to an end. Healing needs to take place in order to break strongholds and to create change toward positive behaviors and healthy relationships. I have come to the realization, not judgment, that many in the family did not get the correct blueprint to follow. They are following patterns of learned behaviors with a mix of their own. Self-reflection, accountability, and honor will help with the healing process to end these cycles.

The Grace of God has kept me throughout the many painful moments, heartbreaks, disappointments, challenges, and life lessons learned. God has anointed my life. I have always had a zest for life. Self-motivation has helped me accomplish a vast number of goals and skills. As a young child, I craved for more, helping others and wanting happiness for them.

Gone are the days of people-pleasing, looking for validation and love, allowing abuse and boundaries to be crossed. I have learned to know my self-worth, love myself, have self-respect, and to always put myself first. Toxic relationships are no longer tolerated or accepted. Peace is what I seek and maintain. It would have been a great bonus to share experiences and to create new memories with my father.

God gives us free will to create the life that we want. It is all about the choices we make each day. I choose LIFE. I choose PEACE. I choose to set BOUNDARIES. I choose LOVING ME.

I have forgiven my father years ago. I do not know much of his story. Perhaps he will find peace and healing for himself. My father is living with the choices that he made. Each day that rises, my father is living life on his terms. He is living life without having a relationship with his adult children. This may just be what he wants. As the saying goes, "You can bring a horse to water, but you can't make it drink." I have unconditional love for my father. At this point in my life, I have accepted the fact that I may never see my father again. I am okay and I have moved on from the pain, disappointment, and abandonment. I wish my father well and may God bless him. It is a sad reality, and it is real. My siblings and I are beautiful human beings, who are IMPACTING this world through our gifts and talents from God. Our father is missing out. We could enrich his remaining years on this planet.

There is an anointing on my life and God wants me to fulfill my destiny. As I reflect over my life, I am thankful. I am grateful for the Grace of God. God has strengthened me through every hardship, untruth, disappointment, hurt, and pain. My core, my being, has begun to HEAL. I am a SURVIVOR. I am WORTHY. I am STRONG. I am LOVING. I am KIND. I am UNSELFISH. I am LOVED. I am a VISIONARY. I am a LEADER. I am BLESSED. I am a CHILD OF THE MOST HIGH GOD. GOD IS MY FATHER.

My story continues to unfold. It is forever evolving to what God wants me to do. I have PURPOSE. I will continue to IMPACT lives and bring forth my TRUTH, LIGHT, and HOPE.

The story never ends, as long as there is breath in your body. Each day, as you inhale air in your lungs, God is not finished with you yet!

God wants us to be the head and not the tail. Deuteronomy 28:13, NIV reads, "The LORD will make you the head, not the tail. If you pay attention to the commands of the LORD your God that I give you this day and carefully follow them, you will always be at the top, never at the bottom." Always hunger for MORE and take care of YOU first.

God believes in FORGIVENESS and ABUNDANCE. God wants all of his children to attain it. There's room for us all to reach the levels that God has ordained for our lives. STEP INTO YOUR DESTINY. I have come to realize that I'M NO LONGER A FATHERLESS DAUGHTER. I AM GOD'S DAUGHTER.

Rev. Julieta Johnson, MS, a native of Panama, Central America, is founder of Unique Gatherings. Her passion is creating safe spaces for open dialogue and courageous conversations for spiritual and personal development. One of her favorite quotes is the African Proverb, "If you want to go fast, go alone, if you want to go far, go together." Her foundation in ministry was shaped as a member of Mt. Airy COGIC for over three decades under the leadership of Bishop Ernest C. Morris Sr. She was Ordained at New Life Church of God by Bishop Stanley Webb and served on the Ministerial Staff for over a decade.

She is a graduate of Cairn University and Eastern University. Rev. Johnson is a retired Faculty of Community College of Philadelphia. She served as a member of the Faith and Spiritual Advisory Board for the City of Philadelphia and a member of The American Association of Women at Community Colleges. Julieta is a widow and proud mother of four daughters: Andrea, Angela, Crystal and Erika.

I Almost Gave Up!

JULIETA JOHNSON

I never thought I would share this part of my story. Most saw me always smiling, poised and resilient. I stepped into this chapter of my life as a 36-year-old divorced mother with two young daughters. I was left on a dark and scary road alone. It happened so quickly. There were some potholes along the way but I never expected a complete detour. I was forced to get off at this unfamiliar exit. I was broken and ashamed. My days ended with me crying out in a fetal position. I was lost and in misery. I could not find my way, and I did not know where to go. I did not want anyone to know. I was angry with God. God was supposed to look out for me and protect me. God let me down. I did not know where to turn or who to turn to that would understand. I saw no way out of this pain that I could not even explain.

Divorced was a title I did not know how to accept. It came with trophies of pain and shame. I tried not to use it and did not want it used in reference to me. When my legal decree came in the mail, I hid it. When asked about my husband, I said he was fine or out of town. I did not lie. After all, he was fine and out of my town. I tried to drive the pain away. Once I drove from 4 pm and arrived back home at 10 pm. I did not make any stops. I just kept driving and crying. This suffering was most painful at night after tucking my daughters to bed. I entered a cold room and an even colder bed. I cried each night until my body shook and woke up each morning to heartache. I did very little talking to God, although God kept trying to talk to me. I was devastated, embarrassed and grieving. Grieving in a divorce was worse than death. All the stages of grief were present, but no one physically died. I was grieving because my hopes, dreams, love and what I thought would be my future died. This was similar to the pandemic, death without a funeral. I received no cards, no resolutions, no chicken was fried and no one was buried. Even though I did not send out any announcements, everyone knew. There was no way I would survive this shame. I was a child of God and loved the Lord, but this queen was dying. A paradox consumed me as I looked in my daughters' eyes. I knew I had to find a way to pull through. They needed me. God reminded me that He was there. I was very involved in church. This Junior Church Mother was experiencing suicide ideologies. How could this be? I was so confused. I could not get away from the presence of God, but I was not going to listen to a God that did not block this pain.

I woke up each morning with enough strength to go to work and made sure my daughters went to school. I smiled with a broken heart. I tried on weekends to escape at church. Church was a familiar place. Somehow, I was no longer comfortable in this space. I felt like I was on stage and the topic of every conversation. Everyone around seemed happy and blessed. I would cry out to God, "What about me?" My family was broken, my life was broken, and our chain had a missing link. I had a disease that others did not want. Many would hug or shed a tear when they saw me; most did not know what to say.

I went to church late and left early. I did not want to entertain any conversations. I knew I was in trouble when I looked down at my feet one day and I was wearing two different shoes; they were not even the same color. That night I made a deal with God. I asked God not to wake me up in the morning and to give my parents strength to raise my girls. Well, God did not listen, but I knew this queen was dying. I needed help. I was convinced that I would not survive. I was trying to fight, but I had no strength. I was a failure. I took off my crown, convinced that I would never be happy again. I was immersed in depression. Death seemed so much easier.

One morning I woke up and my pillow was not as wet. I somehow gained strength and came to myself. I saw signs of the next exit, even though it was miles away. I was now able to sleep through the night. One morning as I rolled on the floor in agony, I cried out to God with all the strength I had. I found the courage to reach out for help and attended grief counseling. I was the only one in the room where the one that died was me. I gained fortitude to survive. I was able to make an appointment with a therapist. I froze during my first appointment. I was unable to discuss the detour of my life. My therapist was amazing. He handed me a glass of water. He said we would only talk when I was ready to talk, but emphasized that I needed to talk. I called a week later, ready to talk. The session was painful but amazingly freeing. I opened up to a complete stranger. I felt safe. No one knew. With the help of my therapist, grief classes, and hesitantly talking to God, the next exit was closer.

My new exit was on Afraid Avenue and was not as dark. I did not cry as often. I learned in therapy that I was not a divorcee but that was what happened to me. I did not share my visits to therapy with anyone. Many were convinced that all I needed to do was read my Bible and pray. I read daily and prayed until I had no more words. I wore the OK mask so well that many did not discern my unbearable pain. Although afraid, I started to open my heart. I met several men at that exit and had a few relationships. Even though those relationships did not last they made me feel good again, like a woman again, and attractive again. I was no longer as angry with God, but I was still disappointed with the plan for my life. I didn't know how or when but started feeling that I would love and be loved again and that the next exit would not be as far away.

On an ordinary Sunday morning at church, I sat next to my future husband without a clue. He attended a Men's Breakfast at the Marriott Hotel where he had what he described as an epiphany. God made himself known to him, and he surrendered his life to the Master. He spent the remainder of that day in worship. Upon his arrival at the sanctuary at 7800 Ogontz Avenue, he was captured. He stated, "When I entered the building in a sea of thousands the only smile I saw was yours; I asked myself who is this Nubian Queen? There goes my wife." The plan of God was unfolding, and my destiny sat next to me. He said he asked the Master to bring a queen into his life that he could shower with love. He had several queens before but did not know the Master or how to really love. He was ready now. He had no doubt that the Master would grant his request.

A week later at dinner with his friend he wrote his number on a napkin to be given to the lady he sat next to at church. I received the napkin. I kept the napkin, prayed over it and talked to God about it. Two weeks later I called, and we talked for hours. I was uneasy and cautious. He was strong, confident and did all the talking. We talked every morning and every night. He made me smile; yes, he made me laugh again. We finally went to dinner. The queen put on her crown. I looked up and a 6'4" tall glass of water sat next to me and held my hand. My heart skipped a beat. I was hesitant, terrified, but trusting God and opening my heart. After several months the love of this man embraced me and God winked at me. God sent Love my way and I made the exit off of Afraid Avenue. He was amazing and everything I needed. I was happy and my daughters could see it. I was flying without wings. We were married one year later in the church where

162

he saw that smile and made that request to the Master. The Master answered.

The love we shared was fresh, real and so pure. We honeymooned on a South American Cruise sailing from Montego Bay, Jamaica to Columbia, Costa Rica and Panama. He made each day an adventure. He would drive me to New York City for breakfast and to visit NYU. He studied at NYU and loved New York. We would come back to Philadelphia to pick up the girls for dinner. He loved saying "mi esposa," my wife, in Spanish. He loved speaking Spanish to me, knowing how much I loved the language as a native of Panama. He learned the language while living in New York. He loved my daughters and welcomed them as his own. He had two sons and a grandson. He was not a stepfather and they were not stepchildren. Our home was warm and filled with love. We would play oldies and dance on Saturday mornings. I felt loved. I was so happy. I was no longer angry with God. I thanked God for always being around and surrendered my will.

In the midst of this whole new world, there arose an emergency in my family. My two great-nieces were in need of a home. This was no easy task, as they were nineteen months and four. After six months of marriage, we took in these little angels that we later adopted. We purchased four car seats, diapers and formula. The Johnson home was now a family of six. This took a lot of adjustment for my teenagers and me. Our home was busy but filled with love. The adjustment took time but with prayer and patience God filled a home of tears and uncertainties and transformed it into a happy place. This was both challenging and exciting. Evenings were filled with books and homework. The children were all in school and daycare. I matriculated to Cairn University and my husband was completing his Master's degree in Human Services at Lincoln University. I started all over changing diapers, potty-training, and reading bedtime stories. God provided the daily strength that I needed. The amazing daily doses of love that I received from my husband were also an antidote for my stress.

We are often told to expect the unexpected. Approximately one year into our marriage, my husband developed a strange cough and persistent fatigue. After several doctor visits including the Veterans Administration, as my husband was a Vietnam Veteran, the unexpected occurred. He was diagnosed with Chronic Congestive Heart Failure and Exposure to Agent Orange. *Agent Orange* was a tactical herbicide the U.S. military used to clear leaves and vegetation for military operations during the Vietnam War. I was not sure what all those words meant. I convinced myself this could not be too bad. God would not have me take another detour. God just would not allow that. I started praying and rebuking the enemy. The news was really incomprehensible for me. I tried my best to keep my tranquility, and my husband did the same. I had so many questions for God I was overwhelmed as days, weeks and months moved very quickly.

My husband could no longer work or complete his last semester at Lincoln University. He was scheduled to have bypass surgery. The doctors were hopeful that this would help his fatigue. This queen believed this was the answer. The day of the surgery we arrived at the hospital at 6 am. The doctors explained the procedure and length of surgery; I would be called to pick him up if there were no complications. I received a call within one hour to return to the hospital. I was confused and nervous driving as I cried and called out to God. As I entered the room my husband grabbed me and looked in my eyes. I knew something was wrong. The doctors explained that he had too many blocked arteries, and his heart was too weak to withstand the surgery. He was given six months to live and instructed not to drive.

A heart attack was likely for him. The ride home was forever. We were both silent.

The following days were spent trying to process our conversation with the doctors and not saying anything to the girls. I recited each day that God was a healer. My husband was so encouraging and loving, which really cushioned this part of our journey but did not change the reality. The hospital became his second home. Even though it was challenging becoming his caretaker, raising four girls, still in school and working, I completed each daily task. The prognosis did not look good. I was convinced that God was looking out for this queen and everything would miraculously change. Each day I would claim and believe that this would be the day. I refused to believe what my eyes could clearly see. I cried, I prayed, I anointed and fasted as I waited for my miracle. I reached out to all my connections. Everyone was praying.

I was awakened by my husband one evening for assistance to the bathroom. I could not get him back to bed, and we both fell. I could not move him. My brother came and was also unable to move him. We called 911, and help arrived quickly. The news was not good. His kidneys shut down completely, and he was put on dialysis. I could not understand what was wrong with God. I begged and pleaded with God to do something. I was weak and my crown was tilting. God was not listening. My husband was discharged to a rehabilitation center and then a nursing home. We made the best of the situation. I was there every day. Somehow, I was not angry but still hopeful that God would perform a miracle. Nothing changed. My husband requested a meeting with the doctors. He wanted to stop all treatments after almost two years of no change. He did not like his quality of life. He wanted to give the Master a chance. He was ready to accept the Master's will. I was speechless and still allowing God to be God.

One day as we ate dinner in the nursing home my husband seemed so at peace as he sat up in his bed. He took my hand and told me how he loved me and thanked me for taking care of him. He told me not to worry. He thanked me for the opportunity and honor of being Mr. Johnson. He was no longer as strong. He weighed 150 pounds and wore diapers. His love was unquestionable as he complimented my smile. I was still waiting on my miracle from God. There was something different about his countenance. I fed him and anointed him. He held me so tight.

Later that evening his son came into town. Even though it was late we went to visit him. Upon our arrival the nurse held me and took my hand. He slipped away to be with his Master on December 31, 2003 at 12:01 AM, right before we arrived. I screamed, cried and called out to God. I was numb and speechless. I got in his bed and begged him to wake up and not leave me. He did not wake up. It was a long ride home. My daughters tried to comfort me. I arrived home emotionless, wondering how I would make it. I cried myself to sleep. I asked God, "Why am I alone again?"

After the funeral, telephone calls, and visits, reality set in. Heartache greeted me again. The girls and I would hug and cry. I told them that God would take care of us. Those were just words. I was both sure and doubtful. I was not sure that I could defy the anger, pain, and suicidal ideologies I was feeling again. I did not want to be alone. The odds seemed to be against me. Voices in my head told me I would not survive. How could God love me and allow this? I fought and prayed and called out to God daily with everything within for my sanity.

God is real. One night as I sat on my bed, I felt God's presence. I was immersed in "a peace that transcended all understanding." My shackles of doubt were loosed. The chains of defeat were broken. I had an epiphany. God promised to never leave me and assured me that He was always there. God is faithful. God did perform a miracle. My husband is with the Master. My crown is straight. The girls are all college graduates. This Queen defied all odds. I had five years of amazing love; God had a plan. The experience was worth every tear I cried, and every pain I felt. The grace of God even allowed me to rekindle friendship with my first husband, who transitioned one year ago. I forgave him and was part of his home-going. I remain open to the will of God, Ephphatha!

Linda K. Brown, Founder/CEO of Fully Unleashing Life, Incorporated, a nonprofit, 501©3 and Fully Unleashing LLC, a for profit organization. The non-profit's mission is to help people know their purpose, and to educate, encourage, equip, and empower women and teen girls, because everyone is "perfect for their purpose." The primary focus of the for profit is transformational life coaching and counseling. Both raise awareness of the importance of mental health among teens and their parents in black communities, providing education and community resources to build relationships to perpetuate the awareness.

Linda is a certified life coach, licensed mental health counselor, and ordained minister. Linda is a graduate of the Leadership Training Center of Impact Church, Jacksonville, Florida. She has a MA in Counseling from Regent University, Virginia Beach, Virginia and a BS in Interdisciplinary Studies (Psychology and Music) from Norfolk State University, Norfolk, Virginia.

Being & Becoming on Purpose

LINDA K. BROWN

You would think since this is my story, facts, and events about my life, that it would be rather easy, simple, a breeze, to share, right? Well, not really. So many thoughts went through my mind about this process, and it is just that—a process: where to start and what to share because the ultimate purpose of sharing my story is that it would be an encounter that will bring hope, healing, encouragement, and empowerment. Also, it was truly not coincidental that I called my friend Cheryl at the same time she said God had placed me on her heart to reach out to, to be a part of this anthology and talk about God's purpose and timing for my life. And I thought of abandoning this mission several times along the way, procrastinated a lot, but ultimately, I know it's a part of the journey. So I pray as you read this, and the other stories shared in this book, you will get exactly what God had in mind for "just you." There is purpose with destiny here for you. This is the story of the **"Enters"** of my life, and my journey through them.

There are so many directions this story could take to talk about the various life imprinting times that literally shaped and reshaped me as I moved through the various stages. The first was my actual birth itself, a miracle, because my mother had to have a cervical cerclage, a surgical procedure, after three miscarriages; this helped hold me in the womb until it was time to be born. **Enter codependency.** Then, at eighteen months, my mom shared that as she was unplaiting my hair to wash it, lumps of my hair fell into her hand: **Enter the disease of eczema.** It ravished my body, and my earliest recollection was at age three being covered in scale, looking as if I had been burned, dark rash patches all over my body, some cracked skin with blood peeking through from me scratching to relieve the itch and annoying uncomfortableness of it all.

Sitting on the porch of our new home in a new neighborhood, I was playing—banging, because I couldn't really play—my toy piano I'd received as a Christmas gift, and singing, enjoying my time, although every now and then I would hit some pleasantries. There were two little girls on the porch next door. They were gazing over at me, but I did not really pay too much attention. My mother came to the front door, and they asked a question: "Is it catching?" I wasn't sure what they meant, but my mother knew right away and responded, "No," and told me to come inside. I went inside and I don't remember my mom's exact words, but I do remember her encouraging me that everything was all right and to not be bothered if children in the new neighborhood did not want to play with me. **Enter rejection; not feeling accepted.** That is what I felt and connected the dots that it was because of how I looked. **Enter insecurity**, and I lived with these and so many faulty thoughts and perceptions for years.

Fast forward to age 26, and I now had four children, and realized I was stuck. What sparked me to begin to think this way was when I was taking my newborn son to a doctor's appointment and I looked at myself in the mirror. It was a shocking view. I had my hair parted down the middle in two ponytails and bangs, bobby socks rolled down with sneakers, skirt, and blouse (I was in a church that dictated women could only wear dresses and skirts; that's another subject for another time). I thought and said to myself, *You look like you're 16 but you're 26 with four (4) children. Why are you still dressing this way? What's going on with you?*

I was sixteen and a teen mom, which was life-changing and traumatic. **Enter shame,** piled onto all the other entrees in my life... simply too much. It was traumatic to be pregnant at 15 and giving birth at 16, a devout church girl, dad on the deacon board and mom the founder and president of the first ever deaconess board of our church—just wrong, as one of the mothers of the church put it. So then how do you keep going and really live?

Well, 26 was the age that I started to think about my life differently, and I decided I didn't want to stay stuck. So I began the journey to becoming a woman, a mother to my children and a wife to my husband. After all, being a wife and mother were two of my most burning desires. I so wanted to be chosen, accepted, and loved. And just as important, I believed it was a huge part of my purpose and destiny in life. Besides, I had a great example in my parents, who modeled a great marriage, 26 years together before my dad passed. An aha moment too: As I'm writing, I realized that they were married for 26 years and here I am at 26 taking a different view of my life...interesting. Of course, I had never heard them fuss or fight. Although one day I thought they were fussing, and I started to cry. My mom asked what was wrong and I said, "You all are fussing." She replied, "No, we're having a discussion, we're not fussing." And that was that. But my life would be a rollercoaster for so many years and I would struggle with the **Enters**—how to deal with and dismiss them from my life.

As a licensed mental health counselor, I have had the privilege of studying psychology and counseling, which I really loved, and the importance of mental health along with the effects of mental illness on a person's life. It was during my graduate work that I realized the things that had happened to me had brought me to a place of depression; that I wanted to get things done and get to my destinations expeditiously; and I had a rather low tolerance and was impatient and hypervigilant. I later discovered that I suffered from seasonal and situational depression for years and much later I realized how hyperactive I was, easily distracted. There was a time I remember going to the doctor because I was stressed out, and they said they wanted to put me in the hospital, but I told them I would come back, and I never did. I would have been put on the floor for evaluation of my mental status; I had four children that I had to care for, and I had no one to rely on to take care of them for me. The suffering continued but not without me trying to help myself.

If I may be honest, I didn't really believe that I had any mental health issues, and I really believed being saved, sanctified, and filled with the Holy Spirit would do it, and take care of anything. If I prayed enough, read my word, was righteous, went to church—you get the picture—everything would be all right. Well, that wasn't the case for me because the main thing that was left out was the practical application of what I was reading from the word of God, really allowing my mind to be transformed, then believing in the prayers I was praying, and letting go of the past, vital to moving forward. So I set out to help myself even more. I reached out to a friend and my neighbor, who invited me to a weekly prayer service in her friend's home. I attended as often as I could, trying to pray away my troubles, but I didn't replace the thoughts that were causing me to feel the way I felt, so my behavior was the same. I didn't know how to believe the prayers to change my situation, *for real*. I knew how to go through the motions, crying out to God, but not to really give my problems to Him and let Him do the work in me. My journey continued.

As long as things were good, I was good, on the surface, but I would worry about things. My marriage was always a rollercoaster of events, up and down, and it was draining. But it was the one thing that I so desired and I knew I was made for. I am assured that God gives us purposes and one, as I mentioned, was being a wife, but it was the one area I struggled in the most. I often put my children before my husband and that was out of order. Then I would live in the past, bringing up things from the past, such a source of contention. And ultimately, my marriage ended for the second time, to the same man. **Enter not enough, not in my purpose.** However, here is where my journey shifts to being and becoming, and this time being and becoming Linda. For the first time in my life, I was without children, husband, or family near me, just me. I lived with friends for a few years, something unfamiliar, having only lived with my parents, husband, and children in our own spaces. I now live all alone, first time ever, and I have discovered that in this process, I'm enjoying getting to know Linda. She's very cool, cute, calm, collected, comical, constant, and cuddly. She's a woman, worthy, worshipful, wealthy, wise, witty, and simply wonderful; that is who she is! And I really mean it.

But how did I get to the point of saying, feeling, and believing these attributes about myself, the girl of dependency, disease, insecurity, rejection, shame, and not enough, not in her purpose, you ask? Well, it is a journey that I'm still on, during the process of trying to pray everything away without practical application of the word of God in my life or going to therapy on a regular basis. I left that out; I did have therapists on this journey. Nevertheless, I learned so much. I was good at giving out advice, scripture references and helping others to begin practicing the word, believing in their prayers, and taking responsibility for their actions, but I would allow the weight of the situations or circumstances in my life to override what I knew to be true. I was trusting myself and other people for my deliverance and not God – **remember codependency** – dangerous and very unproductive. Codependency is when you have difficulty making decisions and identifying feelings, valuing the approval of others more than your own, and lacking trust in yourself and having poor self-esteem. Oh, I failed to mention I had almost no self-esteem due to my insecurity for a long time. But God is our "real security." In Mark 12:31, He really meant what He said: to love Him with ALL your heart, soul, mind, and strength. Why? Because He really will come through when others won't; He's not a man that He would lie, nor will He have any false pretense with you. Therefore, the way we come into total reliance and dependency on God is trust. It is challenging when you're a fix-it yourself type of person and taught to be independent. It's hard to allow God to have total control of your entire life – BUT it is POSSIBLE!

So I want to talk to three people during the rest of my story: little girls, teen moms, and budding women like me who may suffer with codependency, insecurity, not-enough syndrome, rejection, shame, and even the ones who think they are the ugliest person alive. First, please know that your thoughts are so important. Proverbs 23:7, KJV says, "As a man thinks in his heart, so is he." Of course, the man is mankind, men, women, boys, and girls. Furthermore, Dr. Wayne Dyer said, "Your thoughts are seeds that you plant." Jesus said in John 6:63 KJV, "...the words that I speak unto you, they are spirit, and they are life." Therefore, the words are seeds that will grow when planted and they will take root in the acceptable place they are planted in. The phrase, "Sticks and stones may break my bones, but words will never hurt me" is incorrect. I would rephrase it like this, "Sticks and stones may break my bones, but words that are not accepted by me will never hurt me." You see, when you believe what is spoken over and into your life, the planting begins. As you continue in acceptance of what has been spoken, the words take root, and they will grow. It is only as you realize you've believed and accepted a lie that you must pull it up by the root and replace it with another thought/word, thus stopping the growth of what you don't want to grow in your life.

I like alliteration; it helps you to remember, so I use it about who I am now because I really believe the words I'm writing and speaking. This helps to reinforce my belief by saying these words and each word beginning with the same letter is easy to remember. I accept who I am, why I exist, and who I am becoming. I am whole, healed and even being healed as I really take thoughts by saying words, like what I shared "c's and w's;" affirming and confirming who I know God created me to be. It was His intention for me to be, to live fearlessly and wonderfully, being accepted in the beloved. As a little girl, the scarring from the disease kept me feeling ugly and not accepted, even though kids did ultimately start playing with me. It was what I thought they were thinking as well as my comparing myself to my friends that kept me in this state. There is no room in this life for any one person to ever compare themselves to anyone else, except yourself; you are unique, one-of-a-kind. Even multiples have their unique qualities that distinguish them, set them apart from their siblings. The name of the company founded by Dr. Mels Carbonell, "Uniquely You," sums up God's idea of us. You are "uniquely you," and you are "perfect for YOUR purpose", the motto of my non-profit, Fully Unleashing Life.

The things that entered my life and I allowed to linger, fester, grow, and have a crippling effect on my life were simply words. And the words were only able to do what they were intended because I allowed them to be in my life, grow, and develop. This is revelatory even as I write, so good too. "Biology gives you a brain. Life turns it into a mind," says Jeffrey Eugenides. This is such a true statement. As believers, we have another option: We go from having our minds to having the mind of Christ—best mind ever—so we have the ability to think like Christ thinks—amazing. It is up to us to do the work to have His thoughts, which are words of spirit and life, that can manifest in our daily endeavors as we put them in, meditate on them, get help when we are having issues with this process, and know the difference.

Believe it or not, everyone struggles with something, says Dr. Rheeda Walker in her book *The Unapologetic Guide to Black Mental Health*. She goes on to share in her childhood, certain things were not talked about, children stayed in their place, "out of grown folks' business." I heard that growing up too. And the thing not talked about was any sign of mental instability. It had, and still has, a stigma in our communities. Also, she noted few people in the black communities feel they have someone reliable and trustworthy to call on. In other words, we don't want our business in the streets. But everyone has stuff. In fact, Jesus told us this was a part of life in John 16:33, in this world we will have trouble. He went on to tell us how to deal with it: Be of good cheer; He's already taken care of it for us—what has happened, what is happening, and what will happen. It is left up to us to really believe that, act upon that, live that…and it includes getting help if we're having challenges. He said we are to help each other out when we see someone struggling and also bear the burdens with them, and I'm adding not with anyone else.

So if I were to speak with the teen moms out there who have accepted the thoughts of shame, missing a part of your purpose, I would say know there are no accidental births—all are purposeful. The little one you brought into this world has something that only she/he can do. And the real shame would be that if that life you added to the world, as well as your own, full of purpose and unrealized potential were not lived purposefully. Furthermore, the people you were destined to meet along your purposeful journey would not receive what they needed from you because you didn't be or do who and what you were created to be or do. Meditate on this!

Going on to speak to the budding woman, who's struggling with transitioning from a teen to a woman, maybe stuck, afraid or even suffering from any of the things I've mentioned as my struggle, or something else – you're enough. Be diligent to go after every thought, every word that has been spoken over you to keep you in your struggle. Pull it up by the root, and plant life-giving words so you can live and do life on purpose. God is for you! Nurture your soul and prosper as 3 John 2 admonishes; that's what I'm doing.

Leslie Crudup, MBA

It was not until she discovered forgiveness that Leslie found her calling...with the passing of her mother, Beatrice Webb.

Forgiveness became the foundation of who Leslie is today. She has devoted her career to what she identifies as her breakthrough, transforming lives thru mindfulness and relying on her interests in Buddhism and Enlightenment. She is a Certified Life Coach, Public Speaker, Author and Business Mentor. Leslie Crudup, a native Philadelphian, was raised in the Germantown and is the proud mother of a 12-year-old daughter and wife to a wonderfully supportive husband!

Leslie obtained her Life Coaching Certification from the Health Coach Institute, an ICF-CCE accredited program. Today as Owner of LCrudup Coaching she helps others with redefining their lives thru her signature program, **Beaxtraordinary: A Transformation Project.** Leslie helps people who are frustrated and unsure of their next steps redefine themselves, much like she has done herself!

When I Learned About Forgiveness

LESLIE CRUDUP

It is April 2021, and I am eternally grateful. I am not sure how I made it to this side with the ability to smile at all. A few years back my world was crumbling around me, and I was certain I would be submerged in the ashes with no sign of reviving myself. I have basically started a new life and today I am just grateful, and I can certainly say that faith and perseverance will help you find your victory. EVERY TIME!

Here is the thing. I do not consider myself a spiritual person per se. I do not attend church often and I am not at all as well versed in the Bible as my grandmothers (both of them) would expect. I have been baptized and I do believe in the strength of the church community. I grew up in the church, sort of. I attended church as a child but as an adult my mother left the decision to me to pursue spirituality as I saw fit. She was raised in the church as a child as well and as she raised us, she did not attend church. She would get us dressed, give us money for the altar and send us on our way with my aunt, every Sunday. In my mind she believed in a higher being. I suppose she already had her conversation with Him; it was now my turn!

Back to the present day: It is important to me that you know something about my mother because this story is about how she and I finalized our earthly relationship. By that I mean that my mother passed away and my last months with her were the most poignant in my life. Little did I know the events leading to her passing would be the PIVOTAL turning point in my identifying WHO I REALLY AM! It took me this long to figure it out!

My story is driven from my experience with discovering and coming to terms with my mother and her illness and managing the family dynamic that spiraled like a tornado as each of us came to terms with my mother's plight. My siblings and I were at odds and while there was clearly no doubt that we each loved my mother tremendously, we clearly experienced my mother's unraveling differently. Having different experiences, we adapted differently. We each had our own perceptions of what would be considered best care for my mother. This continual discord caused a ripple in our relationship as siblings. As water penetrates a rock, over time the rock may maintain its overall shape but clearly the changed crevices and indentations are evident and permanent. Throughout the entire ordeal I was, however, fortunate to have my husband and my daughter as my lifeline. They remained in my corner and provided a haven for me to decompress on a daily basis. I am eternally grateful. And now I have been invited to participate in this amazing opportunity and allowed to share my personal story.

Here is where it all began. The year was 2017.

And so that ended my phone call with my real estate agent. I hung up the phone and I cried. This beautiful home that I was so in love with was about to be put on the market because I could not afford it any longer. When we took on this home, I knew it was going to be a stretch. I remember how my hands shook when we signed the closing papers. How was I going to afford this home that was almost double the size of my existing home? But I wanted and needed to move out of my current neighborhood, and I wanted to change the dynamic of my life. I convinced myself that I was taking a step outside of my comfort zone for the sake of my family. I figured if I could just get past a couple of years, we would be ok. My husband was never for this idea. He wanted to stay where we were, but I was a dreamer, and I thought a stretch would be tough, but it would then be okay. That final phone call sealed the deal. We tried but we could not keep up with the payments, so it was inevitable that it was time for us to move. This was devastating to me and one of the lowest points of my life. I was embarrassed, I was depressed, and I was mortified. I felt like I had come so far and now it appeared without much of a notice I was being dropped off a cliff.

Moving in with my mother was not in my realm of thinking and even if it were to cross my mind, I would immediately expunge it. I love my mom but moving in with her would never be a consideration. I consider myself an independent woman, after all. I got myself in this mess; I will get myself out. It was my sister and my brother who brought up the idea of moving in with Mommy. I remember the conversation clearly. I remember feeling like something about this was going to go horribly wrong. I could not shake it. I think that is why today I have tentative feelings about my relationship with my siblings, specifically my sister. I wanted to blame them for talking me into this idea. I know now this choice was no one's but my own.

Against my better judgment and especially against my husband's, I convinced myself that maybe this could work and so we prepared for the transition. My husband and I did not want to leave our home. We had other expectations and we were prepared to find another place to live. The deal, however, was sealed after we had conversations with my mother. She did not hesitate and thought it would be a nice change as well. She had been living in a huge house alone and she and the house could use the attention. I think she was even more excited to be in the home with her granddaughter. Simone was seven years old at the time. I remember at the kitchen table the day we decided, I was still caught in my feelings. It felt like a nice idea but still not a good one! Why, oh why did I not think that this was a great idea?

And so we moved in with my mother. It was only a matter of time before we realized there was a storm brewing. During our own grief and loss of our home, my mother was in the midst of her own loss, that of her mind. Little did we know, my mother was suffering from a debilitating disease known as dementia. Dementia is a deterioration of the mind as we know it. So easily hidden it was, this dementia. Shortly after we moved in, before we even emptied our boxes, dementia hovered over the home like a black cloud. My mother's mood and demeanor changed almost seemingly overnight, and we were NOT about to live with the person that I knew and loved as my mother. It was not even the person that we talked to across the kitchen table. What I thought was going to be a great opportunity for my daughter to bond with her grandmother and an opportunity for us to bond as well turned into a nightmare.

I grew up in a two-parent home. My mother and father were both instrumental in raising all of us. Each played their own part in our rearing. My mother was the lead in being the matriarch and prominent parent in most cases. To set the stage, I will say that my mother and I got along beautifully all the years of my life until this day. I already mentioned her position on religion. As a woman, Mommy was hardworking, resilient, and incredibly resourceful from childhood into adulthood. As a young woman she worked as a buyer at a major department store, and she was always seen impeccably dressed and was a rare beauty to many. She did EVERYTHING herself. She made dinner every night and would sew until wee hours in the morning making her own outfits to wear to work, sometimes the very next day. She prided herself on being an original in everything she did. Her clothes were always one of a kind, her home was elegantly decorated with the latest style, and she kept a well-run, tight kitchen about eating. Her kitchen counters were to always remain spotless! We were used to Mommy, of course. We just knew the golden rules. Never sit on the living room furniture, do not leave dishes in the sink and the snacks in the brown cabinet over the TV were for our school lunches, NEVER on the weekend. She loved us as any mom would. She was not a touchy-feely mom. Her love came in conversation and discipline with a soft tone. She never hesitated to teach us something. She was always a TEACHER and while sometimes we resisted, there were many times we so much appreciated it.

As far as my own relationship with my mom…growing up she was a MOM, right? She drove me crazy and as a teen I was rebellious. I knew she loved me, however, and the lessons I did not learn then I am so glad she taught me anyway. She told me about making sure a boy loves me a little bit more than I love him. She told me to let love come to me and not chase it down. "Let him call you; do not run calling him." She told me to walk fast and carry a pen at work, even if it was to the bathroom. She told me that NO ONE is ever going to tell me I cannot do something. Only I can tell myself that. She would shower me with "momisms" miles long. She molded me even when I resisted. She wanted to give me everything she EVER learned and then some because she loved me so much. Sigh. I could not imagine my life without my mommy…thank goodness she taught me how.

So we moved in, as I mentioned, and things were never the same… EVER. After moving into the home with Mommy, every single day we argued, and we fought over things that made absolutely no sense.

I could not understand why she would accuse us of stealing from her or taking things from her and invading her privacy. None of that was true but it was a battle we could not fight. Every other day my mother was telling us we needed to leave. And every other day my family members were saying that I needed to stay. When I would tell them about how things were going, they would tell me I need to try and get along and make it work. But now to come home every day and to argue with someone who does not want you there is debilitating. My family members were not the most comforting at the time. When I was not arguing with my mom I was arguing with my sister. My brother tried to understand and tried talking to Mommy at times. My sister, however, would not budge and proceeded to be EXTREMELY judgmental in my opinion, and very unsupportive.

The only people who seemed to help me at the time were my husband and a few close friends and a couple of other family members far removed. I could not even call my mother's home my home at this point because my mother did not want me there. All I kept thinking is how empty I felt. I was already out of a home and now I was losing my mother and my siblings were along for the ride.

The only thing that gave me comfort that I really did not expect was writing. I am not and was never a writer at all. I had a diary when I was about 16 but after I left for school that pastime was a memory. However, after commiserating with my husband and/or burning the ear off the closest person I could get hold of, I decided that I was going to just write out my frustrations. I wrote uncontrollably every single morning when I went to work. I would do so before I would open an email. I would write about how I was feeling or maybe even the details of the fight or circumstances the night before. Writing was a release for me. It was a way for me to take all my frustration, depression and anger and put it on the shelf.

As my mother's condition deteriorated, so did our relationship. My relationship with my siblings took a turn as well. Eventually my mother ended up living with my sister and I had to move out just for my sanity. I remember my sister saying very vehemently that she thought I was deserting my mother. I was doing far from that. I was trying to save the relationship that she and I had as well as save my marriage, as well as protect my daughter. I continued to visit my mother every day at my sister's home, even though my sister and I were not on speaking terms. Upon entering my sister's house I would proceed directly to my mother's room to take care of her. Many nights I spent the night with her, sleeping next to her on the floor or in a chair. I did this as long as I possibly could. I did not and do not ask for pity. This was my job as her daughter, and it was what I needed to do.

I remember one night sitting in the room with Mommy at my sister's home. My mother was crying out, as many dementia patients are prone to do in their sleep. I remember trying to get her to go back to sleep. There was a moment...an exceedingly small moment...when she was lucid, completely aware of where she was, and she looked at me. She asked me why I was there lying on the floor. She had the most loving eyes and for that split second I saw my mommy in all her brilliance, her strength, and her vulnerability. It was so profound. I wanted to cry. Only seconds passed and she was again encapsuled in delirium. But what a gift! I was there for that moment. And then I realized.

What did this teach me? FORGIVENESS!

This entire story that played out with our moving in and then moving out taught me more about myself than I could ever know. My mother taught me this last lesson just when I was not looking. I suppose I could call it her last MOMISM. I had to learn to put aside how I felt about my siblings and any support or lack thereof and concentrate on taking care of my mother. I had to look past the disease and know that my mother loved me and that her anger was nothing more than a symptom of something she could not control. I had to forgive myself for arguing back, for taking sides, for being so angry at myself. I had to learn to forgive my siblings for being judgmental and lacking the compassion I THOUGHT they should have. I forgive myself on so many levels and I forgive my sister, brothers, and anyone that I thought was out to harm me. My sister and I said some hurtful things to one another. I had to forgive myself even if she and I had never spoken again. They loved Mommy just as much as I did; we all just lived the experience differently. I cannot do anything about that!

This lesson of forgiveness keeps playing itself repeatedly. It has been the entire catalyst to my change in ways I had never imagined.

I realized that I was not happy with in my career, and I was not happy with my relationship with my daughter or my husband. I knew that a number of things needed to change and unbeknownst to any of us, this had to happen so I could see! There is a question: Is life living for you or thru you?

I decided to leave my job. My mother passed away about three years ago. I wish I had done this sooner so that I could tell her. I thank my mother for allowing me the opportunity to finally manifest into my true calling, to live my life to the fullest each and every day and to be grateful for the gifts I am granted, right here and now! I was like a bird in a cage with a broken leg with the gate wide open. There is no one and no thing that can tell me how beautiful life is when you know true happiness if you let go. All I had to do was fly. There was nothing stopping me.

I suffered loss…tremendously. I had no home, no mom and at one point, no sister. I then went to having no job. Today, however, my heart is filled with love and acceptance. AND I have my sister back (that is another story). I feel more alive in my body than I ever did.

When I was asked to do this book, I was told this was for queens who defied the odds. Initially I did not see myself as either a queen or someone who defied the odds. But then I immediately thought of the story which has been the pinnacle that will play out my remaining life. I get overjoyed and a little weepy about it just writing this.

My life is dedicated to forgiveness, thanks to my mommy.

Desmond Tutu states in his *Book of Forgiveness*, "Forgiving is the innate perseverance of happiness."

Author, Writer, Producer, Entrepreneur, CEO & Founder of God To My Rescue Nichole HB Productions. Nichole is a Domestic violence abuse advocate.

Nichole was born in Cleveland, Ohio, and currently resides in New Jersey. She's a college student at Strayer University for her Bachelor's Degree in Business Administration/ Concentration: Entrepreneurship.

Nichole has traveled throughout the United States and lived in many places. She studied marketing at Penn Foster University, Leadership, and Biblical studies through DTS and Jerry Jenkins Writers Guild's member. Nichole has studied filmmaking through Spike Lee's masterclass and business through Disney CEO Bob Iger. She follows the leadership and ministries of TD Jakes Potter's House, Vineyard Columbus, and Dr. Tony Evans.

Nichole hopes to reach as many people as possible through her books, audiobooks, products, and blogs that show them how to recognize their self-worth with self-care and provide them with unmeasurable insight into God's greatness, protection, and destiny for their lives.

Overcomer

NICHOLE HARRISON

Invite God into your situation and experience joy over the pain. You can overcome any obstacle you face in life. My real-life story here only marks the surface of hardships. I've endured health scares, grief, and bankruptcy. I've been a victim of predatory lending. I've experienced infidelity, abuse, heartbreak, and toxic relationships one after another. To this time in my life, even through all my calamities, I feel peace only God can give that surpasses all our understanding. To this moment, I thank God I made it. I am Nichole Harrison, overcomer. You _____ are an overcomer.

2008 was a challenging year for me after my ex divorced me, my dad became terminally ill and I lost my home as a victim of predatory lending. I lost my job, and then I had to file bankruptcy on top of everything.

Now you'll find out how you're going to make it through this.

1. **Psalm 121:1-2, NIV** I lift up my eyes to the hills. From where does my help come? My help comes from the LORD, who made heaven and earth.

Then you're going to see how you're going to get your strength back.

2. **Philippians 4:13, NIV** I can do all this through him who gives me strength.

Then you'll know you're going to live through your calamities.

3. **2 Corinthians 12:9, NIV** My grace is sufficient for you, for my power is made perfect in weakness.

You can rest assured God's got your back! **2 Chronicles 20:9, NIV** "If calamity comes upon us, whether the sword of judgment, or plague or famine, we will stand in your presence before this temple that bears your Name and will cry out to you in our distress, and you will hear us and save us."

God is our source and our strength; He will not let us fall apart. He will always come to our rescue. He has given me everything back and more than what the devil stole from me. We will overcome any adversity that comes our way when we trust in the Lord.

Psalm 46:1, AMP "God is our refuge and strength [mighty and impenetrable], A very present and well-proved help in trouble."

Let me be transparent for a moment. I struggled for a while with knowing my self-worth. I thought sex would make a man fall in love with me and want to make me his wife. I thought if I gave him what he wanted, he would change his cheating and manipulative ways.

I thought I could change a man's thinking pattern using sex, hoping that would work out somehow in my favor. Then I thought somehow I could change how he manipulated me into buying him gifts or giving him money, hoping that doing these things would make him love me, but once he got what he wanted, he went MIA. Yeah, I was that girl. I was hoping I could change his lying behavior. I was hoping I could change his deceitful practices.

I must admit I was naive, but God showed me that I couldn't change anybody. I can't change a man's thinking pattern or behavior or hope things will get better. Once a man shows you that side of him, believe it. The man has to want that change, and that was bigger than me.

Sisters, we are God's masterpiece because He created us without any consent from anyone else as to how we should look. We are created in His image, not man's.

It is time to see yourself through a different pair of eyes, ladies, where God sees you. Recognize your worth in a way where others can see you and notice something different about you, not being arrogant but confident in knowing you are the daughter of the King of Kings and the Lord of Lords. From the crown of your head to the soles of your feet, you are beautiful, dark, light, white, big, medium, or small. Men will begin to see how you carry yourself and if that's the man God has for you, he will follow God's lead to love you, respect you, care for you and protect you, his blessing, his queen.

I thank God I don't look like what I've been through in my life. Never judge a book by its cover. Behind someone's smile, you never know what they're going through. No one would have ever guessed the things I went through behind closed doors because of how I look on the out-side. The abuse, depression, heartbreak, and pain I've endured... The only difference between then and now is that I know my worth. God has always supplied all I needed. If I had just listened, things might have been different. But we all go through something, and God's strength is the only way to make it through without breaking. God wants us to listen to him and follow His direction for our lives. He gives us free will to make our own choices, but when we choose to do things out of God's will, we have to deal with the consequences of our actions. That's why it's essential to read the Word daily and meditate on it so that we can apply it to our lives daily. You have to pray that God's will be done in your life. Pray for wisdom when making decisions that could change the trajectory of your life. But you see, that's why God never leaves us because He knows we need Him. I don't carry the weight of abuse, depression, and that type of pain anymore on my shoulders.

I now know my worth, whereas before, I didn't. I've been saved for many years. I was saved when I was abused, I was saved when I was depressed, I was saved when I was in pain, and my heart was breaking. But I didn't know my worth. I thank God for a new day, a new beginning, and a new life where I can share and help others along the way. I am, and you are, a vessel full of power, a treasure from the Lord. Thank God today for His strength and His power within you.

2 Corinthians 4:8-9, AMP tells us, "We are pressured in every way [hedged in], but not crushed; perplexed [unsure of finding a way out], but not driven to despair; [hunted down and persecuted], but not deserted [to stand alone]; struck down, but never destroyed."

For that thing or that relationship that almost took my life, it could not because God has great plans for me just like He has for you.

Jeremiah 29: 11, KJV "For I know the plans I have for you, declares the LORD, plans to prosper you and not to harm you, to give you a future and a hope." You see, what the enemy meant for evil, God has worked out for our good.

You see, God's plans for our lives never changed from the beginning. God has never been confused about how and what we would go through and how we will get through it. The Lord's strength is what we need. He expects us to rely on Him to get through troubled times and unbearable situations. He always knew that I would be able to get through the pain. I am still here; you are still here. I am still alive; you are still alive. I'm still blessed, and so are you.

If you are going through something that seems unbearable, trust and believe God will never leave you nor forsake you. He will make a way out of no way in your situation, even when you can't see it. When you can't see God in action, He is still working things out on your behalf in your favor. Just trust Him and believe.

Are you or have you ever been a victim of a Silent Abuser?

Not all emotional abuse involves screaming or judging. More common forms are neglect or paying little or no attention as well as carelessness or oversight or stonewalling. Through my research, here's what I've found out.

"I describe stonewalling to clients as to when one person turns into a stone wall, refusing to interact, engage, communicate or participate. Much like what you'd expect from a stone if you were talking to it!" (Relationship researcher John Gottman, PhD).

Have you ever felt?

1. Unheard and or Unseen
2. Unattractive
3. Walking on eggshells

Verbal Abuse/Red flags/Signs

1. Blaming, Threats
2. Raging Violence and Impulsive Aggression
3. Name Calling-Profane, Derogatory
4. Circular Conversations-Arguments that happen almost endlessly, every day or every other day, with no resolution
5. False Accusations
6. Hysteria-inappropriate overreaction to bad news or disappointment, which diverts attention away from the real problem and toward the person who is reacting
7. Belittling and Condescending – This kind of speech is a passive-aggressive approach to giving someone a verbal put-down while maintaining a facade of reasonableness or friendliness

Unlike physical wounds, which heal naturally, leaving scars, this is terrible; however, verbal and emotional wounds left untreated tend not to improve. These scars are hidden at times and become a part of who we are and how we act. Physical injuries hurt us; verbal and emotional wounds go to the deepest parts of us.

The injury which comes from verbal and emotional abuse is a severe condition, and if you don't get the proper help for it, this can become a fatal injury. I was a victim, but now I'm an Over-comer, a Victorious Soldier in the Lord's army! Here's how I found my plan of escape. Are you ready to find your plan of escape? Trust God in the process and get the help you need today. Call on the Lord, and he will deliver you.

Psalm 34:17, AMP "When the righteous cry [for help], the Lord hears and rescues them from all their distress and troubles."

I can do all things through Christ who strengthens me. The Spirit of the Lord was with me through that ordeal. I am strong and of good courage and will not fear, be dismayed, shaken, nor lose courage. I am not swayed if things look like they are not working or if something doesn't happen tomorrow, for I know only good things come to those who love the Lord. It has to happen; as I say, my peace is still. That's why I study God's Word to find out what He has promised; that's where I find the courage to share my testimonies with you. For each situation I face, I find the courage to share my testimony. I encourage you to do the same, whatever problem you're facing. It's not always comfortable, but trust God through the process. Go to Him in prayer; He's always ready to listen. The burdens you carry, you don't have to carry alone as long as you invite God into your situations; He will walk with you along the way and bring you out on the other side according to His perfect will and timing. Don't try carrying burdens on your own. We were not equipped to take certain things, but God can handle everything. I choose to be of good courage and let the Holy Spirit guide and direct my path, trusting and believing suitable for my breakthrough. Trusting His Word, praying in the Spirit, believing the Word of God! He's genuine, all-loving, and all-powerful, and His promises are true. Don't be discouraged. Don't be dismayed; call upon His Name, the precious Name of Jesus.

John 16:33, ESV "I have said these things to you, that in me you may have peace. In the world, you will have tribulation. But take heart; I have overcome the world."

But I am of good courage, confident and sure of what I believe and undaunted by it all; for Jesus has overcome the world we face every day and has deprived it of its power to harm us and has conquered it for us.

Say this with me: I am born of God, so I am victorious over this world, and this is guaranteed by my faith in Jesus Christ and His finished work for me. I no longer think I cannot get out of a situation, because I have the courage and I understand the Spirit of the living God is at hand, ready to assist me in whatever I need to do. He is going to bring me through to victory.

Psalm 103:2-5, NIV "Praise the LORD, my soul; all my inmost being, praise his holy name. Praise the LORD, my soul, and forget not all his benefits—who forgives all your sins and heals all your diseases, who redeems your life from the pit and crowns you with love and compassion, who satisfies your desires with good things so that your youth is renewed like the eagle's."

Eight years ago, I lived in Atlanta, Georgia, and I would leave for work during the week at 6:00 am. While I was driving to work, I thought about what I was experiencing in my marriage and the best escape plan—consistently thinking, *Lord, how can I be set free from this verbal and emotional abuse driving me mad?* I couldn't quite figure out how I was going to get out of this marriage. Once again, I made a vow to be married and stay married before the Lord and to my husband, I wanted to honor my vows and continue with the union, but it was so toxic I knew if I stayed, I wouldn't be here today. I began having a panic attack driving along the way, so I pulled over. At that point, I started to cry out to the Lord. *Father, please get me through this. I need your power and strength to get me through this,* I thought to myself as a child would. For example, imagine a child walking beside his or her daddy for a moment. But somehow, the child got lost in the crowd. A stranger approaches the child and says, "Come with me now!" in a stern and threatening tone of voice. The person tries to grab the child.

The child then gets away, begins to scream "no," and starts running and screaming through the crowd for his or her daddy to help and save him or her, along with saying, "Help, a stranger is after me!"

Then the child sees his or her daddy and runs toward him, with Daddy's arms open wide, ready to receive his child into his arms. The child at that very moment sighs in relief, knowing that he or she is now safe in Daddy's arms.

Proverbs 18:10, NKJV "The name of the Lord is a strong tower; The righteous run to it and are safe."

That's exactly how I felt when I ran to God for safety, away from an unhealthy marriage that tried to take my life. The Lord once again walked me through these overwhelming, tragic events, then delivered me from the snares of my enemy.

Psalms 27 1-5, NKJV "The Lord is my light and my salvation; Whom shall I fear? The Lord is the strength of my life; Of whom shall I be afraid? When the wicked came against me to eat up my flesh, My enemies and foes, They stumbled and fell. Though an army may encamp against me. My heart shall not fear; Though war may rise against me, In this I will be confident.

One thing I have desired of the Lord That will I seek: That I may dwell in the house of the Lord All the days of my life, To behold the beauty of the Lord, And to inquire in His temple.

For in the time of trouble He shall hide me in His pavilion; In the secret place of His tabernacle He shall hide me; He shall set me high upon a rock."

I used to sit and look at couples in different places and based upon their facial expressions or engagements of happiness with one another, I would often think to myself, *They must have a great relationship. They look like they have a wonderful life, or I wish I had a relationship or marriage like theirs*, or merely thinking, *They look great, so great together.*

Even though some couples do have excellent relationships or marriages, the bottom line is, every couple has struggles. But it's the way to handle those struggles when they come at you. You have to go in agreement together with the Word of God and with Him leading the way. Make an effort not just to say you're going to make changes but also to put them into action. Pray about your relationship issues and struggles. When you love God and yourself, you will be more inclined to love your spouse or the person you're in a relationship with and others. Love doesn't hurt, envy, or boast. Love is not rude, proud, or self-seeking. Love is patient, and love is kind. So whatever struggles you are having in your marriage or relationship, if you love that person, you will work together, compromise, and make sacrifices to tackle whatever it is you're facing together, with God leading the way. But if you're not on the same page or are not willing to work together through hard times, keeping God first, your relationship will never be complete and filled with all that God has in store for you together. Sometimes people have to separate to keep the peace and have peace of mind.

Our mental health is essential; it's best to take precautions before getting involved too deeply with someone or forming a relationship too quickly. Spend time with the person and get to know them long enough to see their characteristics and personalities, likes, dislikes, and make sure you're compatible. If you're around a person long enough, they'll eventually show you who they are, and believe them when it shows. Then you'll know your next move. Don't take this lightly. It's okay to have fun and enjoy a person's company, but be cautious and safe. Please don't base your decision to be with a person on their looks or money. Don't get caught up in false images or material things a person can give you. Don't build a relationship on false pretenses; it doesn't end well and can be deadly if you don't get out in time. We never can imagine what a person's motives are or what someone may have experienced in their life to cause specific behavior unless they reveal it and get the help they need, if need be.

When people looked at us, I'm sure they may have very well thought the same about us that I used to think about other couples (how great they looked.) They didn't see the mask that I was wearing for the public to see. Behind closed doors, the mask came off. I was sad and depressed.

They couldn't see the verbal or emotional abuse and neglect I endured behind my closed doors. But now I'm set free. Remember along the way, God's timing is not our timing. Trust and believe He knows what He's doing and what we need when we need it, whether you're in a relationship, single or married.

Whatever it is you're dealing with, God will see you through it. Be patient and listen to the Lord's still, small voice as He prepares you. Get ready to walk in your deliverance God has for you.

Galatians 1:10, ESV "For am I now seeking the approval of man, or of God? Or am I trying to please man? If I were still trying to please man, I would not be a servant of Christ."

2 Corinthians 10:12, ESV "Not that we dare to classify or compare ourselves with some of those who are commending themselves. But when they measure themselves by one another and compare themselves with one another, they are without understanding."

Keep the faith. Trusting God's process through our daily living and challenging times allows us to experience the peace of God on a whole other level—His unconditional love, happiness, joy, and peace. Inviting God into your situation takes your faith to a whole different level where you'll receive blessings, miracles, favor, and increase that only God can give. Believe God when He tells you He will never leave nor forsake you. God bless you, overcomer.

Shonda McCants is a resident of Philadelphia who grew up in environments where she should have died. Life was tough but with Jesus Christ she is victorious. She has taken the difficult situations she has faced in life and turned them into fuel to ignite her fire to help others. She pushes through life believing that her story can and will change the world one person at a time!

Shonda currently works as a life coach where she utilizes her education and life's experiences to help people overcome adversity. She passionately believes that everyone has the potential to be the best version of themselves but ultimately the choice belongs to the individual.

Shonda has never met the standards of "Normal" and has always danced to the beat of her own drum no matter how many people disapprove of it! Her goal in life is to share her story through many aspects of ministry to help others heal from the inside out and become their true selves. She is freedom, she is strength and she is change!

Resiliency and Me

SHONDA MCCANTS

Dear Shonda,

I write to you today to first tell you how beautiful, amazing, strong and courageous you are. You have weathered some severe storms that almost cost you your life. You allowed the rejection and abandonment that you experienced as a child to dictate to you that you were not valuable, worthy or accepted. You let the loss of your childhood determine who you were, and that led you down paths that left you empty on the inside. Every time you did not receive the love you so desperately needed from your mother, you not only hurt others, but you also hurt yourself. You did not allow love in because it was not coming from the source you needed it to come from. You rejected acceptance, you rejected peace and you rejected happiness because your trauma told you that nothing else and no one else could mend your brokenness.

Growing up with parents as drug addicts took away your security and being a surrogate mother to your siblings took away your sense of self, often leaving you hopeless. Let us not forget the countless times you watched your father beat your mother to cope with his insecurities, lack of love and countless other imperfections. Remember how you thought she was so weak and vowed you would never let that happen to you? What you witnessed planted a seed of anger that took root and even when she finally was strong enough to leave it meant nothing because the seed had already begun to produce a harvest. So it seemed like everything was going to be normal for a change but something inside of you knew that even though it was best for your father to go, things would never be the same.

So here comes this man, your father's best friend, and in your mind, he was better than what you were used to because he stepped in and helped your mom get cleaned up and she was happy. To see her smile eased some of the pain of the previous trauma and you could be a kid again, so you thought! Remember how he looked at you? It was weird; whenever you were in the room his eyes would follow you. You did not think much of it, so you continued to be you. Until that day, the day everything would take a drastic turn. You were about 10 or 11 years old, and he snuck in your room that night and touched you. It was not a touch a child should have receive from a man who was supposed to be with her mother. It did not feel right and why did he duck when you woke up? You first thought maybe it was one of your siblings who hit you because there were a few of you in the same bed. You then figured that could not have been the case because you slept with the younger ones, and none of them had a deep voice, nor were they old enough to cuss. So you realized you needed to tell someone, and you did, but telling cost you everything. Oh, how you wished you had just kept it to yourself. Maybe life would not have shifted the way it did for you. Not only were you called a liar but that is what you were pegged as. Not only did you have to live with the shame of having your innocence violated but you also had to live with the lies that he spoke over you that you were fat and not good enough. Let us discuss when you ran away, and you thought you were free, but they made you go back to live in what in your mind was a living hell. You ignored his advances, dressed like a boy and even lived in the shame and pain of being torn down by a man who had an unhealthy sexual obsession with you. So yet again you attempted suicide because no one else was willing to save you.

No one believed anything you said, and it seemed as if the whole world was against you. Your behavior continued to become violent, especially in school. Your teachers just thought you were "bad" but never imagined that in order to be safe at home you had to fight a grown man. It appeared that you were outnumbered just fending for yourself up against everyone and the lies they spoke over you. You know those lies came from how you behaved, right? No one was interested in why you were so angry; they were only interested in rewriting your story to fit their narrative. Shonda, I know not many people told you, but you were brave! You struggled because your voice was stolen, and you were left to protect yourself. This caused you to become louder and to vow that no one would ever silence you again. Little did you know that that vow would cost you healthy relationships, not just with outsiders but even your siblings. Remember the pain you felt when they called you the same names he called you? Remember how you took that pain and devalued yourself? How you took the rejection and vowed you would make everyone pay for what you went through.

Finally, you gained the attention of the system and finally they were giving you your voice back. You got to choose: stay in a house where you felt unwanted and unloved or go to a place that would bring you happiness. You figured hey, they would not take you from your God-mom; she was the only person who understood you, the only person who accepted you and loved you. They would surely see that being with her was the best place for you to be. Nope, sorry Shonda, another derailment that would set the course for more pain, rejection and anger—this all because of the jealousy of a mother who thought that someone was stealing her child and lack of care from a system who half-did their jobs. Devastated you were when you found out your choices were to go home or to a group home for children with behavioral issues. You chose the group home, but you took it hard. Remember you felt like your mother hated you so in turn you hated her too? You wanted them both to die!! Again, you were left feeling like she did not protect you when you were little, and she was not protecting you then either. So what did you do? You made another vow and that vow birthed RAGE! You wanted everyone to pay for letting you go away; you wanted them all to pay for leaving you alone in a place with strangers who did not care anything about you. None of them visited you, nor did they call. You died internally that day and nothing was ever the same.

Abandonment gave life to Nikki, your persona that was out for blood, and it did not matter whose it was. Someone had to pay for your pain. Nikki was your protector, the destroyer, and she stopped at nothing to get vengeance for what happened to you. Together you two made a vow that you would fight your way through everything and reject the very thing that you so desperately desired: LOVE. You fought when people called you names, you fought when you did not get your way, you fought when you were embarrassed, and you fought when you were emotional. No one could contend with the rage that was inside you. You sold your soul for revenge and it led you to some dark places. You forced the home you were in to reject you and once that feeling entered in, the only thing left to do was to hurt someone else and after you were done, hurt yourself. So you beat that girl until you could not beat her anymore and when staff intervened you beat them too. Once the damage was done you grabbed the largest knife you could find and locked yourself in the bathroom because this time you were going to finish what everyone else started. You felt there was nothing more to live for, no one wanted you, no one understood you and no one loved you!

Wake up, Shonda, and look at what you have gotten yourself into. Now you are in a mental institution and these people really think you are crazy, so much so that it stuck. Crazy Shonda—that is not what they called you but it was a label you decided to attach to yourself. Another drastic measure to keep people from loving you. Here you are in a place you would have never imagined yourself in, all because she snitched. This was not even your fault, at least that's what you told yourself. You struggled with taking accountability for your actions; you thought that what you went through was a good enough excuse to be the way you were. Days went by, then weeks, then months and you sat and watched people come and go but no one was ever there to get you. You did find companionship before you went into that place. Remember that guy you met at the park? You thought he was so cute. You did not even care that he was 25, which was way too old for you. You were only 15; what did you think you were getting? Let me guess—someone to love you, right? Wrong! You thought he loved you; he was always there even in that place. Remember he pretended to be your uncle just so you could talk to him? He was the only person who called for you any way; you found security and acceptance in him. He said all the right things to make you smile; he said he would never leave you and he would always love you. Words you held tight to, since it seemed like no one else did. You were in a place where you could not go to the cafeteria, you could not go outside, sugar was banned, and you could only receive one phone call a day and even with all of that going on he was willing to be your "knight in shining armor."

Being in that place so long brought your leadership abilities to the surface. You were able to effectively communicate how going to the cafeteria, going outside and receiving more than one call a day could cause behaviors to decrease. The doctor was able to hear you out and give it a trial run and it worked; all of them caused a decrease in behaviors, which allowed those rules to be incorporated indefinitely. Your voice was finally heard, and it not only helped you but it also helped those around you. It made you feel good to be listened to—temporarily, that is. Nothing was able to compensate for watching people come and go and you still be stuck there with feelings of not being wanted. This rejection and abandonment were the fuel that caused the flames of rage and hate to grow inside you.

Here comes the day you have been waiting for; it is finally time to go. Someone wanted you but they did not really mean anything to you because the fire had grown too large to put out with such a quick fix. You should have been happy and leaving with a sense of accomplishment but instead you left with a power that fed the new identity that you decided to embody. So here you are, a force to be reckoned with, and you have not even made it through the door yet. Your record painted you to be a monster, a juvenile delinquent who was unlovable. No one wanted to know the real you; they could only see the traumatized you, the hurt you, the rejected you. They only paid attention to the "Crazy" you, a name you were willing to live up to in order to prove to people that you could be exactly what they wanted you to be. They did not care anyway, so why be vulnerable? Why show them your pain? Just be the lies they read on paper is what you said. So Nikki arrives full of rage, full of hate, building your arsenal so that no one would hurt you ever again. You went on a rampage; you attacked everyone who came your way, even those who wanted to love you, and that did not matter because everyone was considered a clear and present danger. You lied, stole, manipulated and fought your way through—by any means necessary was your plan of action. Hurt everyone that you encountered was your motto and remorse was not an option. Although you were empty inside and wanted so desperately to be loved, you could not show people that side of you because if you did then it meant more rejection, and that was something Nikki vowed would never happen to you again. You did not realize that you were making things worse; you were making yourself a target and every action seemed to seal your fate.

Things got worse when your sister was murdered by the same system that was supposed to reunite the two of you. You were finally going to be with someone you knew loved you, and they took that away from you. You wanted to die so bad. You just could not wrap your head around why every time it seemed like love was coming to rescue you it was snatched away. June 10, 1997 was the day you died and you fully embraced Nikki. I know the pain was just unbearable but at least you were going to be reunited with your family. You would think that would have changed your perspective on things, but it did not; it made things worse. Once you were reunited you found out that the monster did more damage, and this time there was nothing you could do about it. You were not there to protect your siblings. You left them and now it was your fault that they had to experience a horrific childhood. You took on a responsibility that never belonged to you and lived in torment daily because you knew there was nothing you would be able to do to fix this. You were broken yet again by life and there was nothing inside you that desired wholeness. More vows were made and they all collectively began to overtake you. The disheartening part is none of the vows eased your pain.

All the pain followed you through early adulthood and things got even worse. Now there was no one to tell you what you could or could not do. Drugs, alcohol and sex eased the pain temporarily, low self-esteem plagued you, rejection became second nature, and rage is what controlled your mind. You were spiraling out of control and there was nothing anyone could do. You could no longer hold things together. The dam had broken and you were drowning in hate, rage, resentment, unforgiveness, and bitterness. No one was able to stop the torment. You loathed everything and everyone, and that included God. You could not figure out why He would allow this trauma to happen to you. The more people offered Him to you, the more you rejected Him, and that was because you believed He rejected you. You wanted to know what type of God would allow you to be rejected and abandoned by the ones who were supposed to love and protect you. You wanted to know why everyone including God hated you. Why were people constantly leaving you? What could you have possibly done to deserve such a childhood? You were a hopeless, distraught little girl who was trapped inside a broken, defeated adult.

Do you remember that woman on your job you could not stand? Did you even know that she was interceding on your behalf even though she knew you wanted nothing to do with God? Then on a cold day in November you decided to open your heart to receive Jesus as your personal savior. That was the day your life changed and the process of healing began. This was not an easy process. There was so much you had to recover from and so much fight that had to be removed from you. Each day was painful; each day you had to learn to let go, forgive those who hurt you and forgive yourself. You went back and forth with this process and there were even times you gave up. Through it all you experienced more pain, more trauma and more suicide attempts. By this time, you had a husband and three children who also became victims of your childhood trauma.

You finally decided that you were going to give God everything you had wholeheartedly because you were tired of bleeding on the people you said you loved. You inflicted the same pain onto your family, so surrendering to Christ and forgiving yourself was the only way you could be made whole. It was time for you to receive God's love, God's grace and God's forgiveness. Did you ever think that you could heal? Did you ever think that you could be set free? Did you ever think that there was someone out there who loved you more than life itself? Thank you for allowing God to change the narrative, build you up and equip you with the necessary tools to help heal and set free M.Y.S.F.Y.T.S just like you. Your purpose was greater than your pain, Shonda, and now that you understand that God's plan was perfect, you can finally accept that you are not rejection or abandonment but you were chosen and you are an overcomer. You are not your childhood trauma; you are by the grace of God Making Your Story Fashion Your True Self!

Marisa Miller is a tenacious and goal-oriented young woman from Indianapolis, Indiana. A graduate of Indiana University Bloomington, she is a member of Alpha Kappa Alpha Sorority, Inc. Often smiling and laughing so vivaciously that others next door can hear her. Marisa thrives on enjoying her life. Doing so is her way of worshipping her Almighty God. Marisa believes she can serve others by ensuring they have joy every single day of their lives. Embracing joy was the greatest way she overcame losing a dear loved one. She wants others to experience this same blessing.

Currently, Marisa holds her Master's in Education and is pursuing her Ph.D. in Psychology. Someday, she aspires to counsel families and young adults, specifically in adapting healthy thinking patterns. She also hosts a podcast in which she speaks weekly about past experiences or current experiences that have showered her in wisdom, often in a humorous manner.

Mental Health Crisis

MARISA MILLER

A caterpillar decomposes its old body parts to transform into its new image. Its undesirable traits turn into wings, antennae, and even its beautiful décor to create the free butterfly we see. The funny thing about this process is that the human eye can't see this transformation occurring. It all happens while the caterpillar is enclosed in its chrysalis, isolated from the outside world, silently suffering and experiencing turbulence. As humans, we often look at that jubilant, colorful butterfly and admire it for its freedom. We admire how it flutters so freely in the wind, seemingly fearless and unbothered. However, we often overlook the journey it endured to get to that point. We overlook the identity crisis it must have experienced, or its inability to escape darkness for days at a time. I say this all to say my life represents that transformation. Better yet, my mental health journey represents a woman who suffered silently for years, losing parts of herself and experiencing the highs and lows of life itself, feeling trapped in emotional bondage, and not having the energy to escape it. So when you see my exuberant smile today, when you hear my laughter from seven rooms down the hall, when you see me hopping on a stage without restraint to perform a song, when you witness me making conversation with strangers like I am ready to love them forever, when you watch a recording of me walking across another graduation stage to get another degree, please understand that I took a long, winding journey to get here. Please understand that it took years of prayer, releasing myself, retraining my thoughts, revealing my innermost thoughts to a therapist, staying up at night to reflect, leaving relationships, throwing out my phone, repeating "You are valuable" in the mirror thousands of times until I believed it, and much more. This introduction is just an idea of what I am about to reveal. I have never allowed myself to be this vulnerable before. And quite frankly, I am uncertain how my loved ones will take it. But what I DO know is that my testimony broke shackles off my feet. So if my testimony liberates you, the reader, along the way, then the sacrifice is well worth it!

The interesting thing about mental health disorders is that they don't just appear. They manifest over time and worsen as patterns of thinking change. The process is similar to a cancerous growth: It starts out small, and then spreads to other areas of your body. In my case, depression and anxiety started out small, and spread to other areas of my life as I became older. At 12 years old, for the first time in my life, I felt detached. I loved my family, but I felt detached from the outside world. Hearing that lighter-skinned girls were prettier, not having the best clothes due to a limited income, being taught that everyone is not my friend, and seeing unstable relationships around me really made me feel like an outcast. Specifically, I remember feeling like I looked "different." Compared to other girls, I felt masculine because I didn't have the silkiest hair, my nose was wider, and I was very skinny. I literally used to hold my head down when I walked in rooms. It was rare for me to walk in a room and look people in the eyes. I hid and was usually the first person to leave the room. I was always ashamed of myself. After taking a picture with someone I almost waited for the "ew" comment or the request to take the picture again, with me in a different angle or lighting. I was beyond self-conscious. I simply did not like my appearance. It is so true when they say that confidence is something you wear, because I certainly wasn't attracting the boys I wanted at my age. It's not because I was "ugly." It was because I wore my shame on me. No one is attracted to someone dead. So I stayed away from my peers I considered attractive or popular because I didn't feel like I measured up.

To add insult to injury, finding a "real" friend group was nearly impossible for me. I didn't really want one. Ironically, 12 and 13 years old is the developmental stage where adolescents dream of fitting in with a peer group. My household was raised not to trust the outside world. We were taught that people will let you down. We were taught that your God, your family, and yourself were the only people that you could count on. It was most important to be a leader rather than a follower—to stand out from the crowd. I remember my mother always telling me that she felt like the black sheep of her siblings. She always felt different. As a girl, when you hear these things, you unknowingly adopt this same mindset. I started feeling like the friends that I did have had a hidden agenda and were not as mature as I was. All that said, since I spent so much time alone, I was left to explore who I was. That included sexual explorations. I just wanted to feel wanted, attractive, worthy, accepted, and accompanied. I felt like if I rejected boys' advances, they wouldn't dare even look at me anymore and I would always be alone.

When I lost my virginity, it wasn't a romantic experience, or even a pleasant memory I look back on. It was with a boy I barely knew, who said "make it home safe" when we were finished. This is my first time exposing this. So it's bringing emotions as I type these words. I lost the most intricate part of me. My very being. And kept living life as though it never happened. I keep it buried so deep because I feared going insane if I thought about it. I grew numb at such a young age. I so badly wanted just to be loved that I tried the same experience with the next boy and then the next boy. I will never forget sitting on my front porch one night and my mother opening the door. She asked where I had been. I told her a lie, and I will never forget the pain that I saw in her eyes as I told her that lie. She knew I wasn't being truthful. She saw that innocent part of me slip away. Instead of feeling loved by these boys, I felt even dirtier. Even more ashamed. Even more of an outcast.

As I became older, these sexcapades slowed down. Growing an intimate relationship with God, rather than an obligation, taught me to value myself. I recognized that my body was not disposable. I recognized that I was not just flesh, or a walking object. I recognized that I was a girl who was suppressing so much and hiding so many feelings in a bottle that I was afraid of opening up for the sake of my sanity. However, I still had work to do. I still felt the need to win love. The next turn in this chapter is going to reveal the adversity that took a toll on my mental health for the worst. It made me question if I even desired to live anymore. I spent a full day shopping with my mother for furniture to put in my new apartment. It was my senior year of college and I was ready to embrace my independence. While shopping for sofas, I received a text from a guy who wanted to hang out. Thereafter, I began rushing my mother to hurry. I wanted to go home so badly, so that I could shower and get ready for my date. For the rest of our time together, I had an attitude. Again, I needed to appease the men around me or I would be rejected. I had to fulfill his desire, rather than doing what I wanted. I needed to make a boy happy, rather than spending time with my mother. When I finally got home, I got dressed and darted out the door.

The next morning, I woke up to screams. It was my mother. I ran in the living room to where she was, and begged her to tell me what was wrong. She kept screaming, "My head, my head. I have a headache." She said this four times and passed out. I panicked and called 911. As I sat in the chair in the same emergency room as my mother, I had no idea what to think. After a few minutes, the doctors told us that she had blood on her brain. My stepdad let out a noise that I did not understand yet. I asked them to explain what that meant, and the surgeon painfully looked at me and said, "She's not going to have any quality of life." In my state of denial and ignorance, I didn't take this to heart. My family declared that we would keep her on life support. I just knew that my mother was going to wake back up again. I knew that we would be talking again and in a few hours she would tell me how she was feeling. She would come back home and everything would resume as normal. We would finish decorating my new apartment with furniture, she would see me thrive in my senior year, she would make her holiday meals when I and my sister Brittany came home. I had no idea how drastically my life was about to change. How my whole childhood was about to get stripped from me. How the very woman who was the center of my life was about to slowly slip away into another realm.

Days went by in the Intensive Care Unit. So many of our family members came. We all prayed and spoke her recovery into existence. Having them around gave me so much comfort. I honestly thought this was a temporary situation that we would overcome. For days, all I saw were tubes in my mother's nose and a trachea tube in her throat. When she finally opened her eyes, I felt like I had gotten her back. Until we realized she could not speak. When we realized she could no longer speak, this was the realization that everything was about to change. For two years, my mother was vegetative. Week after week, I saw her lose an essential part of herself. She had to be fed through a feeding tube, she was hooked up to a breathing machine, she could not move on her own, she could not tell us how she felt. Seeing my mother like this was extremely traumatizing for me. She was my everything. My best friend. I would do anything to protect my mother and to nurture her. Internally, I battled the hardest fight ever. I wanted to be right by her side to let her know I would never leave her. To let her know that I would always love her the way that she loved me and Brittany. I wanted to let her know that her baby girl was right there to watch over her and comfort her. At the same time, it was so hard to watch my mother deteriorate, day by day. There was nothing that I could do in my human strength to bring her back. I felt so helpless, confused, and overwhelmed. How could a woman who was so God-fearing, so loving, so nurturing, so selfless, so vivacious, so radiant, so energetic, so positive, so full of life be robbed of her life? Do you know how hard it is to know that your mother is in pain and there is nothing that you can do to ease her physical pain? Do you know how hard it is for your mother to be in pain but not be able to speak to let you know the pain she's in? My mother couldn't scratch her head if she needed to. She couldn't blow her nose if she needed to. She couldn't adjust her leg if her muscles started hurting. My mother lay there, lifeless. Her muscles started breaking down. She had ulcers. There is much more but I cannot get through this chapter if I allow myself to think about it all.

The only reason my family held on is because we had faith that she would recover. We were not ready to let her go. It took me a long time to forgive myself for keeping her in that condition. My mother would not have wanted to live like that. Why was I that selfish to keep her here, knowing the pain she was in? I felt ashamed of myself. I had a strong feeling that my family was ashamed of my decision too. They never said it, but I always felt that tension after the fact. After two years of watching my mother in this condition, we knew that it was time to let her go. It was time to free her of that pain and anguish she silently experienced for so long. The doctors took her off her breathing machine. I sat in the room with her with my family as she gasped for air, a traumatic memory I will never forget. I held her hand as her life passed on into another realm. I did not know if I was relieved that she no longer had to suffer, or lost without the woman who was my everything.

After my mother passed, I found myself wanting to be coddled again. I wanted to be loved, and comforted, and nurtured by a man who would understand. That internal void was still inside me, waiting to be filled. There I was, trying to grieve, and falsely thinking I would be able to grieve by finding a man who would embrace my pain as his own. I spent time with this gentleman, sharing thoughts that I should have kept to myself, telling him all about my mother, crying on his shoulder, and being my most vulnerable. He seemed to be there for me. He seemed to love and embrace me for me. I later found out that he was married. He blocked me and never spoke to me again. Shortly after, I got in a relationship with a verbally and emotionally abusive felon. I remember him laughing when I told him I felt hurt by how he treated me. Months later, I fell for a man who didn't reach out to me on Mother's Day to see how I was doing. At that point, I was suicidal. I felt so abandoned, so neglected, so rejected and abused. I knew that it was time to seek therapy or I was not going to make it. I remember my therapist vividly unfolding my life. His questions brought all my insecurities, all my dark secrets, all my fears, all my guilt, all my shame to the surface. I did not realize that I battled with anxiety and depression. I did not realize that my willingness to share my body stemmed from a need to feel seen and wanted. I did not realize that my attraction to emotionally unavailable men stemmed from unhealthy familial relationships. I did not realize that the guilt I faced about the smallest things stemmed from keeping my mother alive even though she would suffer. I did not realize that all these events in my life took the ultimate toll on my mental health.

After so many years of mental anguish and emotional torment, I told myself "NO MORE." I realized that I would disappoint my mother if I continued to live my life that way. I realized that I was not honoring her by dishonoring myself! She was too amazing, too brilliant, too precious for her life to not be celebrated. My mother overcame so much as a young woman herself. She survived and escaped a physically abusive relationship. She overcame two major heartbreaks. She went back to college to earn her Bachelor's degree. She served God like none other and lifted up everyone around her. She laughed to no end. Even more, she raised me and Brittany to be strong, resilient, fearless women who would take on the world unafraid. From that moment, I knew that it was time to carry out her legacy. It was time to honor her! Most of all, it was time to transform into the woman she raised me to be!

I started taking steps, day by day, to restore myself. Honestly, I took steps to reinvent myself. I learned how to value my appearance by no longer comparing myself to other women. I rejected notions of "lighter is prettier and silkier is better." I learned to make real friendships by surrounding myself with women who had similar goals as me. I learned to live life freely by starting to travel. As I interacted with different cultures, I felt my joy rise to a level I had never seen. My laughter grew stronger and my smile grew bigger. I learned to value my future by studying what I had a passion for: inspiring youth. I learned to value my body by saving myself for a man who God says "yes" to. I learned to value my mental health by valuing my overall existence as a human being. After reading this chapter, I pray you realize what I came to realize: My trials made me who I am. My shame, depression, anxiety, guilt, torment, emotional bondage and self-deprecation turned into my self-love, freedom, jubilance, joy, fearlessness, and passion for life. Just like a caterpillar, I used the pain that I suffered silently to become a testimony for many others to look up to. I pray that I save another life. I pray that I save anyone who suffered silently like I did, and set them free.

Lisa Bernard is married to Timothy Bernard. They have been married for 16 years and have been together for 31 years. They bring together a total of six children, plus two additional children that have been added to their household to care for.

Lisa is employed full time as a caseworker. She works with families that are dealing with some sort of abuse and trying to change and improve the lifestyles of their families.

She leads worship once a month at her church and also works with the children of the church. She also enjoys enriching the lives of those around her, as many people call her the caretaker. She loves to cook big meals and she also assists in the Soup Kitchen at her church.

Lisa has been on several missions' trips to Mexico and Kenya and has a goal to return again. She aspires to write her personal story about the trials she has endured.

She loves being with her grandchildren and being able to enrich their lives and do many exciting things with them.

Lisa's biggest goal is to follow the things that God puts before her whether she feels she can or not, remembering that, if God gives it to her, he will take her through it.

Perseverance Despite the Anguish that Lived Inside

LISA BERNARD

Let's begin with the dictionary definition of perseverance and anguish, then the biblical verses I feel fit the closest to what I was feeling and going through. **Perseverance** means: continued effort to do or achieve something despite difficulties, failure, or opposition; the action or condition or an instance of persevering; steadfastness.

Anguish means: severe mental or physical pain or suffering. Through the Bible I found this passage: "Be assured that the testing of your faith [through experience] produces endurance [leading to spiritual maturity, and inner peace]" James 1:3, AMP. This sums it up for me biblically. Anguish is relatable to this verse for me: "Even though my troubles overwhelm me with anguish, I still delight and cherish every message you speak to me." Psalms 119:143, TPT

My story started when I had split up with my now husband, although I wasn't sure that marriage was ever going to happen, as he lived in my house and I stayed with my mother while we tried to work things out so he would have a stable place for his daughter. Mind you, he had other women in my home while he claimed to be with just me, and

I didn't want his daughter to be unstable so I kept saying to myself, *He will change and it will work out* as my insides crushed every time I heard there was someone else in my home or he went to someone else's home. After a lot of healing and forgiveness, we managed to move past all of that. It was also what God was calling me to do.

One night when I was very tired, around 10 pm on the 17th of October 2004, his daughter called and said that her father was very hot and had four fans on him and said he had a bad headache. I asked if he could get up from the couch and get to the car. She said, "No, he can't get up." I immediately told her to call 911. She called 911 and I met him at the hospital. While he was at the hospital, they took scans and blood work and stated nothing was wrong and he could go home. They were basically treating him as though he was just drunk. I struggled to get him into the car.

It was now about 4 am and I needed to finish paperwork that I was to hand in by 8 am. I sent my boss a text telling her that I needed to get some sleep and would be there before noon. When I got to the house my daughter came out to help me get him in the house. We got him to the couch then I left to go back to my mother's house and my daughter stated that she was going to school. I said, "Okay, I will check on him." I finished my work and when I was done, I called over to the house. He wasn't answering, so I went to my job at about 10:30 the next morning and as I was leaving, the doctor's office called, asking me where he was. When I asked why, they just said I had to get him back to the Emergency Room right away. I stated I was about 10 minutes away. The nurse said, "Okay, I will let them know." I hung up and went back in the office to tell my boss I would need to take the day off. Before I could finish talking to my boss, the doctor's office called back, saying there was a paramedic at my house and if I couldn't get there in five minutes, they would bust through the door. I never even realized how fast I could get across town. When I got to the house my key wouldn't work so I had to use the back door key. Finally, I got inside and woke him. He sat up and said he needed to pee, and he wanted a cigarette.

The paramedic said for me to take him to the bathroom, which I thought a little strange, but I did get him there with them helping to get him to the doorway of the bathroom. He came out and they started asking questions and he started talking, slurring his words and saying really crazy things. He still tried to smoke a cigarette. They tried to walk him out to the ambulance although it didn't work; it took a whole bunch of them to get him out. When we got to the hospital, I realized he had taken me off his emergency contact and had another woman on there, which meant I had no say about anything, nor could I sign for his treatment, so I had to call his sister in Virginia, although she didn't answer. Then I remembered his oldest daughter lived nearby. I was able to reach her and she came right away.

The doctor stated things were critical and they were trying to find a hospital to take him, but he had to remain lying down. Mind you, he was a jokester, so he continued to try and sit up. When I told him the third time to lie down, he started singing, "And lean back, and lean back," from a song. He had all of us laughing, as we didn't expect that from someone who could be dying.

The doctors came over and stated he would be going to Jefferson Hospital. I immediately apologized to my sister, as it was her birthday. She told me it was okay. She and the family stayed with me the whole time and went with me to Philly to meet with the doctors. I started praying and telling God, "I know I might not desire this, but for the sake of my children, please don't let him die." They sent me home and told me to be back at 6:30 in the morning to wait for his surgery, which was a high-risk surgery and the doctors wouldn't make any promises that he would pull through. This was the beginning of me pushing though the anguish of *What will I do? How will I do all this, work full time, take care of my children, be in Philadelphia every day and just have a 'me' moment, which never happens?* I began smoking more than I had been, even though I had been trying to quit. I started experiencing other health issues, but I said to myself, "God has me, I can't stop now. I have too many people counting on me."

It had been about three months since October 18 and now I was dealing with some heart issues. This caused me to stop smoking cold turkey. That next year in January, I had to have a catheterization which caused me to be on Plavix for a year because I couldn't do a stress test and had a lot of heart palpitations and a slight blockage. I worried most about making sure I stayed healthy, as well as having to work full time with families where I needed to be able to give them directives to maintain their families and keep their children at home or assist them with working on getting them back.

Now he was home and all of us, me and the children, now had to work through his mood adjustments: He would have periods where he would state things like I was stealing everything from him. He was going to have me arrested. The children were getting more than he was getting, more attention from me than he was. I needed things fixed in the house and he refused to give me any money to fix them. He also wouldn't remember who I was or where he was, so he would be combative. I would have to be strong, as my children were in their teens and my daughter had to assist me in her senior year. Her teacher was gracious and allowed her to write her community service paper on her father. Family stepped in to allow her to go to her prom, which I was so grateful for because this young lady gave up a lot to help nurse her father back to health with me.

During this time, I lost my home and we had to move. I also had a son who was living the life of the streets and smoking weed. I thought where I moved to, he would not indulge any more, although that is when I learned it doesn't matter where you go, if someone wants to find the weed, they will find it. I would travel an hour every day to go pick up my mother to stay with my husband while I worked and then at the end of the day take her back home.

My landlord decided to raise my rent and I couldn't afford it, so I had to move in with my mother since she was my husband's caretaker. At that time my adult children needed to move in as well, which meant I had to pull the weight for everyone since they were my children. My husband was in and out of the hospital, sometimes weekly, for seizures and some of the other times he had an abscess on the bone they replaced and had to go in to get that removed, and was having issues with his diabetes.

My husband had asked my mother if he could marry me. He knew that he wouldn't survive another surgery. My pastor asked me if I really needed to marry him in order to take care of him and I replied, "No, but I want to." Then we were told the day before our wedding that he would not have to have the surgery, and everyone wanted to know if I would still marry him and I replied, "Yes, I love him." That Thanksgiving we were married and my oldest son gave me away and my husband's cousin held my husband up as he refused to sit in a chair to be married. It was a beautiful day.

The health issues went on for several years. After about six years things started to stabilize and remained that way for about three or four years, when things became a roller coaster again. It was at the end of the year and I had just started a new job. I had been there about a year and a half and then had to be out to care for him, which left me without sick time required to move into the next year and be in good standing with my job. God pulled through again and showed that when you trust Him, he will come through. People from the entire county, not just my department, donated their time to help me. It was unbelievable, especially from people I didn't even know.

In 2012, I received a call that my father was in the Emergency Room and not doing so well. I tried to get him to a point that I would be able to bring him home, although it was even more work for me, as I was still dealing with my husband and his issues and continued to work full time. I didn't have any children in school at this time, which helped a little, although I was finishing college and preparing for graduation for my Bachelor's degree. Well, God stated to give my father a birthday party and I did. He was very alert that day as I prepared him, letting him know I would be away for graduation that coming weekend and my uncle would be checking in on him.

The day I was preparing to leave to go to graduation I received another call that I needed to come right away. My sister and I went to the hospital and waited for my other sister to get there and had four pastors there as we sang and prayed my father home that day. I never made it to graduation, although my mother and my spiritual mother gave me a surprise graduation party with cap and gown and all. God really does restore the things the devil tries to take from us.

It continued to be stressful for me because I could not show much emotion about things or talk to my husband about financial things or things that bothered me due to the possibility of him having stress-related seizures, which would put more stress on me because I was trying to work and keep things afloat.

My husband was finally settled and we had purchased our home. We had my mother come stay with us, and then I had taken my adult children and their families back into the home. I stretched myself beyond my means and had been dealing with depression that they had no idea about. I had also tried to assist a gentleman from church who had addiction issues. I tried to help him stay sober and I realized I couldn't help someone get sober that didn't want to get sober. I had taken a cousin and her family in due to eviction and drug addiction twice, where once my cousin had caused my house to be surrounded by SWAT and totally put my husband in a different place mentally. We then had her to move out and then my other child moved in.

In 2017 I took custody of a cousin's child who stated she wanted to be a mother this time but needed some help so she wouldn't lose her child. This was a big struggle due to family members not wanting to help and telling me not to do it. I battled with God over doing this and God won. This placed me in a depressed state because it went really bad for me financially, not being able to pay bills and trying to remind my husband most of all that this was an assignment from God. I knew he was not ready for a baby but I had to complete what God placed in front of me. My husband is a man who goes along with pretty much everything I would like to do, which is so different from before he got sick, but sometimes he gets very upset when he feels anyone is taking my time away from him or he feels they are using me. Then he begins to feel like less of a man because he can't work and help me out, so that I'm not working so hard.

After I finally got him to be okay with the baby and the rest of the family now being willing to help me, things had been going well until 2019, when my husband became very ill and would not know who I was, or other family members. He would hide in corners, stating we were poisoning him. He wouldn't eat and was losing weight. Finally, we had to place him in the hospital and they have now diagnosed him with Lewy Body Dementia. We finally got him stable again after I had to again take time off because having him in the nursing home was more stressful for me than having him home. I and my son decided that he needed to come home and we would double team to make sure he stayed safe. We went through a time of him waiting until everyone went to sleep and he would escape from the house. This finally settled down and had been going well until I once again decided to help another cousin out and take her child in.

This was ok until three months later her mother and brother needed somewhere to go and I asked my husband and he finally agreed that they could stay with us until they found somewhere to go. They stayed with us and we had a full household, as I had my two adult sons and their families and then myself and my husband as well as the baby I had, and my cousin and her two children. It was a very stressful time, as not only was there a full house of people, I also was dealing with outside critters and rodents in my house.

Finally, almost everyone has moved out and it is just one son and his wife and my cousin's daughter and my other cousin's baby, me and my husband. I look at these trials that I have had to go through and felt at times I was so alone. I can say now that I praise God for these trials as they have made it so much easier to have compassion for my clients I work with. I see the growth from all of it. I would go on women's retreats to try and find some strength to keep going and remind myself that I do these things according to the will of God, even though I don't really see my worthiness to do so, since it didn't seem like I was good enough to do anything but clean the church and help where no one else wanted to. I could never understand why God would have me be in ministry with another church who poured into me and challenged me to fulfill the call on my life even when I have had so much on my plate, and it has me on a roller coaster some days. I would never change any of it because God is so good. I have learned now to say every morning that today, Lord, belongs to you, so whatever you have for me to do or say I'm open to be your vessel. I live according to Philippines 4:13, NKJV: "I can do all things through Christ who strengthens me."

Remember, when you stay obedient God is so faithful to you and when you are overwhelmed then God knows the intention and if you allow him, He moves according to his will, which is always VICTORIOUS.

J. JOHNSON
7626 FRONT STREET
CHELTENHAM, PA 19012